SANT'EGIDIO, ROME AND THE WORLD

SANT'EGIDIO
ROME AND THE WORLD

Andrea Riccardi
in Conversation with
J.D. Durand and R. Ladous

Preface by Cardinal Carlo Maria Martini

Translated by Peter Heinegg

ST PAULS

Original title: *Sant'Egidio, Rome et le monde*

Copyright © 1996, *by* Beauchesne Éditeur

ST PAULS
Morpeth Terrace, London SW1P 1EP, UK
Moyglare Road, Maynooth, Co. Kildare, Ireland

Copyright © Sant'Egidio, Rome 1999

ISBN 085439 559 8

Set by TuKan, High Wycombe
Produced in the EC
Printed by The Guernsey Press Co. Ltd, Guernsey, C.I.

ST PAULS is an activity of the priests and brothers of the Society of St Paul who proclaim the Gospel through the media of social communication

Contents

Preface

In the Acts of the Apostles the story is told of how through a series of fortuitous circumstances Paul met Aquila and Priscilla, and how together they gave life to a small community: a community of prayer, of listening to and meditating on the Word of God, a community of witness and evangelization. Just as Paul, Aquila and Priscilla met as if by accident and got together, I too and many other people in Rome and elsewhere have had many meetings, at times fortuitous, but which shape history. Each one of us, and there are many – both friends and members of the Community of Sant'Egidio – could tell how he or she had encountered this reality, through what fortunes, journeys, and occasions.

I recall, for instance, how towards the beginning of the 1970s I was walking through the streets of Trastevere one afternoon, thinking about a certain laceration in the Church. Back then, immediately after the Council, there was a deep division between those who were focussed on commitment to the poor and the transformation of society and those who were focussed exclusively on spirituality and prayer. And I told myself: there must be a practical reconciliation, some way to unite solidly in one's life the sense of God's primacy, the primacy of the Word and prayer, *and* a practical, demanding, urgent love of the poor, of closeness to people, to the most abandoned persons. And just as I was reflecting on all this, strolling through Trastevere, I saw a young man with a Bible in his hand. And I said to myself, there must be something here. At the time I didn't know who he was. I saw him disappear behind a little door, and even though I felt very curious and wanted to follow him, I didn't dare to. It was only some months later that, once again fortuitously (it happened to be one of the early anniversaries of the birth of the Community of Sant'Egidio), I met with some of its members. They explained what they were up to; better than that, they invited me to see. Then I began to understand and appreciate this lived synthesis of the primacy of God, of prayer, and of listening to the Word; of taking God's Word seriously and, at the same time, of dedicating oneself in a concrete, effective way to the poor; of studying society and its problems with attention and discernment. What happened to me has surely happened to many others in much the same way, whether they later joined the Community of Sant'Egidio, or became friends of it in many different ways, as occurred with Paul, Aquila, and Priscilla.

The Community of Sant'Egidio is something that surely flowed out of Vatican II, but it clearly emerged above all where the tensions and energies originating in Vatican II were in danger of missing one another. In the intuition that I had back then, in the inspiration of the moment, I understood the intuition that yesterday guided the first group of young people who along with Andrea Riccardi have given life to the Community of Sant'Egidio: an intuition that is always valid for the Church of God. If it hadn't been valid, we wouldn't have celebrated so many anniversaries together nor have prayed together so often. This sort of stability, in unadorned fidelity to the Word of God, to prayer, and to the poor, is a sign that this intuition really was a result of the conciliar renewal that was slowly asserting itself.

From the memory of the past, then, we could move on to the present and future. There is a passage of the Gospel that is entirely oriented toward the future: "A little while, and you will see me no more, and again a little while, and you will see me... You will weep and lament, but the world will rejoice; you will be sorrowful, but your sorrow will turn into joy." This describes a historical process that comes and will come, in which there is growth through many vicissitudes and the conquering of countless difficulties and trials. The important thing is that the fundamental inspiration be a clear one, that it always remains alive, shining before the eyes of all who see it. And the Community of Sant'Egidio has grown from those first beginnings; it has lived through many events. Through so many twists and turns it has spread in its charity, in its attention to the poor and to society as a whole. As time went on it broadened not only its particular interests – which were broad to begin with – but also its achievements. I am thinking of the whole ecumenical dialogue that led to the great conferences of People and Religions and to the Prayers for Peace, meetings that have continued and developed the intuition of John Paul II at Assisi in 1986. I think of all the work for peace that has spread, that has disseminated peace and the preliminaries for peace on different continents. I think, then, of all this great development with gratitude to God. I feel thankful to God especially because in this development the Community has never lost sight of the original inspiration that, in my view, is concerned with prayer, Scripture, the poor, community, society.

Reading this book of interviews by Andrea Riccardi puts us into contact with history, with the reasons and problems of Sant'Egidio, in a highly personal fashion. Having read it myself I offer this wish: that the great inspiring principles lived in practice rather than formulated in theory or written programmes – the primacy of God, prayer, and Scripture and, at the same time, the urgent need to be close to the poorest and most disinherited, the desire to renew society and bring it to life through inter-religious dialogue and the service of peace – may all this be preserved intact by Him who alone presides over changes in the Church and keeps them in unity and coherence, that is, the Spirit of God.

The simple experience that I was lucky enough to have had many years ago, telling myself, "Here they pray seriously, they take the Bible and the poor seriously", can still be inspiring. May it guide us through new paths of dialogue, of human understanding, of attention to all people. May it also prove an inspiration for a society that is laboriously searching for new frames of reference. To be sure, there are many social, civic, and cultural parameters already in place; but the Word of God, the primacy of prayer, and the poor will remain indestructible standards that we will always have to confront. So let us give thanks to God, thanks to this whole Community, and thanks too to all the friends who have followed these events and this path.

Cardinal Carlo Maria Martini
Archbishop of Milan

CHAPTER ONE

From Umbria to Rome

A JOURNEY

To tell the truth, I'm not really an Umbrian. I was born in Rome, and my parents are Romans. My father's family, it's true, has lived in Umbria for many generations. They're from Trevi; they live surrounded by olive trees, a middle-class family from a little town, or rather a village that wanted to be a city. I myself have always lived in Rome, except for a period of ten years spent in Emilia Romagna because of my father's job.

In a certain sense Umbria lies just beyond the outskirts of Rome, with its ancient particular traditions, with that landscape of olive trees and memories of Francis of Assisi. But I didn't immediately become conscious of this particular memory: the awareness of that came much later.

My family's origins were deeply Umbrian and religious. One of my uncles, Placido Riccardi, a Benedictine monk, was beatified by Pius XII in 1954. But the later generations of my family have lost this special connection with the religious world of the olive trees, the world left behind by that Benedictine uncle who died in 1915. So I have to say that I'm above all a Roman, and that for me Umbria has been a late discovery.

When did you make this discovery, and what has it meant to you?

It happened in the '70s. The model of St Francis of Assisi has always seemed very important to me. I began to read the *Franciscan Sources*; I travelled a good deal in

Umbria; I found my grandparents' house. I found *myself* in this little world; I went to Assisi. I got to know a Franciscan hermitage founded by a woman, Sister Maria, with ties to Ernesto Buonaiuti (a priest and theologian who was accused of Modernism his friend Angelo Giuseppe Roncalli, who was acolyte at his first Mass, later became John XXIII), it was a place of friendship. And then I really met Francis. At the same time I was interested in the *Rule of St Benedict*, which, as I see it, is a fundamental text for community life in the Church. I think that its meaning goes beyond the confines of religious life. It's also significant for the organization of the church community as a whole, especially for the affirmation of the primacy of the Word of God in Christian life. These texts, these meetings have been fundamental for me.

Have these texts influenced Sant'Egidio?

They've been an inspiration. Francis has been a treasured companion along the way, above all because he wanted to be a layman, living alongside everyone else, in humility, as a "minor" among minors. St Francis stands for the Gospel straight-out, friendship with the poor and, in the last years, dialogue with Islam, at Damietta, with the rejection of the logic of the other-as-enemy that marks the spirit of the Crusades. Francis of Assisi and his story vividly teach us how the Gospel can be the source of renewal for Christian life. But the reforms of St Francis came out of the Middle Ages, from a society that was completely Christian, under a Christian regime. In our secularized and post-Christian world things are different. At times people talk about today's situation resembling that of the primitive Church; but that doesn't seem right to me, because our laicized culture knows very well what the Church and Christianity are. Every century has its own peculiar scenario. We have to continue and at the same time reinvent.

So were the saints of Umbria something you discovered after the founding of Sant'Egidio? Has it drawn upon any other spiritual wellsprings?

To answer that question I need to speak more personally. My family, after the younger generations had left Umbria, became rather secular. My father, who was a bank president, belonged to this tradition. He was connected with Pannunzio's *Il Mondo*, the liberal-leftist secular review. It had a high cultural tone, and in postwar Italy it offered an innovative model in journalism. The atmosphere at home was tolerant, but not religious. Even my mother was rather secular. This was the atmosphere we breathed. My brothers and I made our first communion; as little children we were taken to Mass on Sunday and to catechism class. It was a Christianity without bigotry, not much interested in questions about the Church, and alien to the Christian Democratic party. My father was never a Christian Democrat. He may have voted for the Christian Democrats in 1948, but for other reasons, out of opposition to communism. He was alien to this tradition. Instead, he was a radical, a liberal, and, above all, influenced by the world of finance. He made a cult of work. For him, as for many others, life *was* work; it was professional duty as a banker, with some strong secular talk about honesty in an Italy that was rebuilding after the Second World War.

They talked about the war at home as something very close to us, and I saw a lot of destruction. We lived in an atmosphere of reconstruction, of loans, debts, and the economic boom: I recall this situation in Rome and the Romagna. My father had joined the Resistance in Albania after September 8, 1943 (after the signing of the armistice between Italy and the Allies was made public); later he was deported to Germany. In our house we discussed recent history. We talked about fascism, because some of our relatives had sided with Mussolini's Italian Social Republic. My father talked about the duty of resistance,

13

but also about loyalty to the king. He didn't hide the disappointment he felt on the day Vittorio Emmanuele III fled Rome, September 8, 1943. In our house people also had a taste for culture that expressed itself in a love for books (my father had a well-stocked library). We did a lot of travelling abroad. Personally I didn't like those trips very much, but later on my attitude changed. I wanted to stay at home. I was a rather rebellious and stubborn child, not much inclined to school or home-work. I recall that in 1956 when we moved from Rome to Rimini, and I had to interrupt the first grade in gram-mar school, I didn't want to go back to the classroom. I said that now I knew how to read and I'd get an educa-tion on my own. Yes, in this family where there was a little bit of religion, secular views, and a great deal of work, I was to some degree swimming against the current: I was reluctant to do what was imposed on me.

Did any of the Popes leave a mark on your childhood?

Not much. I vaguely recall Pius XII, because he beatified my uncle in 1954. On that occasion we went to St Peter's. Placido Riccardi had been a monk at St Paul's Outside the Walls. Among his students was the future Cardinal Schuster, the Archbishop of Milan, who later dedicated himself to promoting my uncle's cause. Placido was a holy monk who lived a life of penitence almost in the style of a hermit, even though he was a coenobite at the Roman abbey of St Paul. He had had problems because of a novice who claimed to have visions. He had challenged this sort of visionary piety and had disagree-ments with his abbot. So he was sent to the large and nearly abandoned monastery of Farfa, in the Roman countryside. He spent the rest of his life there, practically all by himself, where he found a penitential holiness.

He was the uncle of my paternal grandfather. This grandfather had a sister who became a nun, aiming to follow the example of her uncle. In any case Fr Placido had died in 1915, and by my day that sort of religious climate was a thing of the past and held no interest for us.

Still, I have clear memories of the beatification ceremony. I was four years old. I remember the body of Father Placido, but it had the face of my grandfather. After the exhumation, in fact, it turned out that Father Placido's face had rotted away; so a wax mask was modelled on the face of his nephew, my grandfather, to be placed on the corpse. And I have a sharp recollection of the Pope's voice on that occasion: it was the first time I heard the Pontiff speak, so far as I'm aware.

So was Pius XII rather popular with the Riccardis?

Not very much, to tell you the truth. We didn't feel much interest in the Pope. The political situation wasn't going very well; we were bothered by the fact that the priests used to ask people in the confessional, "Who are you voting for?" In our house the Pope came in for some criticism. There was the problem of the Christian Democrats, whom my father didn't like. Above all he didn't support Fanfani (Amintore Fanfani, premier of Italy in five governments between 1954 and 1983), because he had nationalized the electricity industry.

Then one day I caught a glimpse of John XXIII riding in a car. I was impressed by him; I had the feeling that he was a good man, which most likely reflected an atmosphere around him.

The origin of your commitment, which came later, doesn't seem to be something that can be traced back to this not very religious environment, except for a certain sense of openness that it had. Is there perhaps some important root-cause of what later happened in your encounter, if not with religion, then with politics?

I was very interested in politics. In Rimini I met the communist world. I recall that our classes were divided up into pupils who were for Moscow and pupils who were for Washington. Rome didn't exist. Just to be original, I said I was for London. A classmate of mine was called Stalin. After 1956 he changed his name. This communist presence in Rimini was part of my early adolescence. One of the first political experiences that interested me, at age fourteen, was left-wing socialism; it was an idea that I liked. In 1963 there was the split in the Socialist Party, brought on by the alliance of the centre-leftists with the Christian Democrats. This split led to the birth of the PSIUP, the Socialist Party of Proletarian Unity. As a kid I took an interest in all of that. I was restless, and perhaps too I was looking for a place to land.

At sixteen I came to Rome, where I spent the last three years of secondary school at a classical lyceum in the centre of the city. At times I even wondered about religion. During this period I began to read the Gospel, but I remained rather unsettled.

In those years, when Marxist culture was so dominant, didn't you run into Marx and Gramsci?

Not very much. I read Gramsci and a little Marx in 1968. A whole generation was discovering them. My main idea was that the world had to change, that you had to question yourself about how to change it, that you had to invent the future, change the rules of the game. More than anything else, that's what people talked about in 1968. I realized then that change was going on, here in Italy, in France, in America. There was something about this that I found interesting and upsetting. In fact, it was in the middle of this whole generational crisis that I discovered the Gospel, a discovery that made me take a critical view of ideologies and ideological systems in general. That's what 1968 mainly meant to me. I put it this way because ideology was the problem of '68. It was – I insist – the experience of a generation. In Rome I went to a "good" school, the Liceo Virgilio, in the historic centre of the city, where the student movement was very strong. It seemed to me an intriguing moment: people had a sort of eschatological feeling, the sense that change was definitely taking place, but in what direction? First of all, you had to leave behind that "bourgeois world" and get in touch with the working class. But what did "working class" mean?

Did this happen for you at the Liceo Virgilio?

No. The talk that went on about the working class was purely theoretical. As for myself, I had the impression that something there was too closed, too rigid and ideological. And then there were so many human problems, quarrels, discussions, divisions...

The debates were too abstract...

Yes, too abstract; and then at bottom it was a way of doing politics that struck me as old-fashioned. While we criticized the Christian Democrats and the Communists, we were running up against the same problems of official political life: roles, power, arguments... Once again, I had the feeling that human beings had to be changed. As the saying went, everything is politics. But there was something that escaped politics. Putting it quite concretely, we had to change ourselves. But how could we do that?

You discovered this concrete approach in the Gospels?

Yes. I talked it over with my friends: what does it mean to change society if human beings aren't changed? I'm deliberately putting it in the highly simplistic terms we used back then. What to do? The West wasn't a model. The model might have been Castro, Che Guevara, Cuba. But what did *that* mean concretely? Then came the invasion of Czechoslovakia in August, 1968: the human face of socialism turned out to be a hard one. At the same time we didn't recognize ourselves in the brutality of the USA in Vietnam. Then there was the position of those who talked about a third way, saying no to both the East and the West. As for myself, I thought that men and women had to be changed. With that in mind I began to read the Gospel, and then the Bible, insistently. I had procured a copy when I was fifteen. But even when I read the Gospel I kept a certain distance from the Church. For me this ancient book, the book of faith, the Word of God, was something that could make it possible to change people. I thought back then: "If we change human beings, we might manage to bring on the revolution. Only new human beings can create a new world."

At this point in my reflections on the Gospel, I was familiar with a whole galaxy of groups known as *Gioventù Studentesca* (Student Youth), whose headquarters in Rome were located in the Borgo Santo Spirito, near St Peter's Square. *Gioventù Studentesca* lasted till 1970. There was a group at the Liceo Virgilio that some of my friends were in touch with. Later on, the contacts multiplied, but still maintaining a strong autonomy, with the Gioventù in Milan. In 1970 the reality of Rome was articulated in various groups, including mine, that didn't share the same orientation as the others. For my part, I thought of '68 and felt the attraction of the Gospel.

Even while remaining outside the Church?

Perhaps a little too much. But, to be sure, the Church seemed far away from me. I didn't like my parish very much, nor Catholic Action. But I felt the need to do something in my high school. So I set up a group of students that met for the first time in February, 1968 in the Oratory of the Chiesa Nuova, which was the sanctuary of St Philip Neri.

But were you aware of the tradition of St Philip?

Not that much, or maybe not fully... St Philip had founded this oratory in 1564 in a church in the centre of Rome, Santa Maria in Vallicella, called the Chiesa Nuova (New Church). Lay people and churchmen met there to "approach daily the word of God in an easy, familiar, and fruitful way". They helped the sick in the hospital and organized a welcoming committee for pilgrims. These and other initiatives, which included historical studies of the Church and fostering the Roman tradition of the martyrs, were coloured by the desire to renew the Roman Church. For Philip, "the Indies were in Rome". Along with many pastoral and social initiatives, there were people then who tackled the great problems of their day, such as the wars of religion and the return of Henry IV to the Catholic Church. After a long history, after the Second World War the Oratory of Rome, under the direction of Father Caresana, a friend of Monsignor Montini (later Paul VI), had become a landmark for a group of young Catholic deputies in the Constituent Assembly. They were gathered around Giuseppe Dossetti and included Giuseppe Lazzati and Amintore Fanfani, who lived in a nearby street. This was the Oratory and the Chiesa Nuova. Fine, but I knew nothing about all that back then. The discussion topic at our first meeting in the premises of the Chiesa Nuova was solitude: how to get out of it and discover other people.

The second stage was getting to know the world "outside", outside the centre of Rome: the working-class suburbs, the world of the poverty-stricken outskirts of the city, the huts.[1] I knew a worker-priest who worked in the hovels near the Cinodromo, at the Ponte Marconi, more or less at the entrance to the highway from Rome to the sea, along the Tiber; and it was there that I began to discover the outskirts. It really wasn't the world of workers in the strict sense; it was the proletarian and subproletarian world, made up of migrants from central and southern Italy or from the old historic centre of Rome, of the Rome of those days, at times somewhat anticlerical and antifascist: a mixture of construction workers, or workers without a steady job, people halfway between a very modest living and whatever it took to survive, caught between marginality, rebellion, and resignation. In the student world the watchword was, "Students and workers united in the struggle!" I replied that the Gospel had led us to discover an unknown Rome. Why? Because we were middle-class; and this Rome known only by hearsay, from prejudices, was the Rome of the outskirts, the place where the women came from who served as maids in our neighbourhood. So we had to go and discover the outskirts. For a middle-class youth, a high school student, it was in many ways a shocking experience. The poverty, the people who lived in the huts amounted to the discovery that the Third World was quite close to us. The deception of the "bourgeois city" consisted in hiding away the poor. People were taking other journeys, through life and the city, and you could live ignoring the fact of their existence.

The worker-priest who brought me there was very marginal. Another priest I knew had personal difficulties, but we had begun to celebrate liturgies together with him. While a sort of pre-Sant'Egidio was being set up, I discovered the liturgical aspect that had been missing in my experience: worship with a strong participation by the faithful.

In reality all this was a brief phase, during which I also discovered the Church: one feature of it was also the world of priests who were going through a crisis and searching for something new. There were also many groups and discussions: the feeling that while the Gospel is enough, you still have to have a minimum of theological culture and to know how to get your bearings. So I began to put together a theological culture for myself: I set about reading Congar, Chenu, de Lubac, Rahner, and a little postconciliar theology. The moment had come to ask myself what the Council, which had just ended, was all about.

So this was a highly personal and isolated beginning?

Rather. I began to frequent a bookstore in the Via della Concilizaione, next to St Peter's, that I liked a lot. I bought books, and my father asked me: "Why are you buying all these religious books?" At my house they evidently thought I wanted to become a priest. But at the end of my studies at the Liceo I registered at the Faculty of Jurisprudence in the University of Rome. Perhaps I wanted to make a concrete choice, but without bothering with banks. Or, more likely, I thought that law might turn out to be useful for the poor. Actually, I don't know what I had in mind.

I gave myself a personal theological education, but I didn't have very close ties with the official Church. At that time I also read the great Protestant theologian Oscar Cullmann, who had been one of the observers at the Vatican Council and whom I later got to know personally. He was interested in the role of Scripture in the life of the Church. I read, among others, the Russian theologian Paul Evdokimov, who served as my introduction to Eastern Orthodoxy. As a group, we were somewhat on the fringe. We used to go to the outskirts of Rome, to a rather poor neighbourhood called Primavalle, where we had our headquarters in a room beneath the stairs in a working-class housing project. The parish priest said: "In my parish I have them all, the non-members of Parliament from the right wing, from the left wing, from the Church". We were the "non-members of Parliament from the Church", or rather, as he said, "the non-members of the Church". It wasn't true, but this notion made the rounds in the parish of Primavalle. The other parish, in the same working-class neighbourhood, gave us space so we could teach the children of the migrants.

So Andrea Riccardi is someone who built up his religious culture and then, gradually, discovered other authors coming to confirm this cultural and existential patrimony and these new ideas. Can we speak here not so much of influence as of confluence?

Yes, I'd say it's just like that. My first interest was in the Bible. Then, as an autodidact, I took an interest in biblical scholarship. Bit by bit I developed a great interest in theology. Congar made an impression on me, above all because of the historical dimension of his work, as with Chenu. Later I read Bonhoeffer. I had begun to learn about Barth, but it was Valdo Vinay, a Waldensian minister, one of Barth's disciples, who gave me a better understanding of his thought in the second half of the '70s.[2]

Confluence? You mustn't forget that I was about twenty years old. I got a close-up look at the crisis priests were going through after Vatican II: were they supposed to be leaders or something else? They no longer had a secure role to play in the Church... During this time I got to know Benedictine monks with whom I talked about the Bible, the liturgy, monasticism, the Church, and the postconciliar crisis. With me was a small group that wanted to find some sort of identity in the Church. We thought, perhaps naively but energetically, that if we were real Christians, the world would be changed and the Church would get reformed. We had an instinctive dislike of the "official" Church, as we called it, because it was too involved with power. Above all it seemed distant, even though it was in Rome. So I felt the need for a theological culture, to understand things better. I had to lead meetings, speak to other people, think about a future. I felt like someone who had a responsibility and who, to confront it, was bound to be self-taught. And I thought that our little community had to enter the life, and spread through the streets, of Rome.

Which Rome do you mean? The Roman Rome, Dante's Rome, the "Rome where Christ is a Roman", or the Rome of Fellini and Pasolini?

Pasolini's Rome, the Rome of the hovels and the shantytowns. In the background of my book, *Roma, "città sacra"?* (*Rome, a "Sacred City"?*), which was published in 1979, I do a critical evaluation of the idea of sacred Rome.[3] I had the idea that this Rome isn't a sacred, but a human, city – and a sick one at that. Rome occupies a major place in my life. I'm deeply Roman, even if I don't have such a strong Roman accent. As for Fellini's Rome, I didn't run into it till later on.

Fellini's Rome is also a popular Rome...

Yes, that's true. That Rome is Trastevere, San Lorenzo; but it came later. The Rome of my youth is the city of the working-class suburbs, the outskirts, its young people, the contradictions of a Rome that's to some extent scarred by the "violent life" of the Borgata Gordiani in Pasolini's *Accattone*. In high school I did a report on Pasolini. What interested me was the periphery of Rome, which for us "bourgeois" was a kind of revelation. A world which was the opposite of ours, but not detached. A human world, violent at times, but also extraordinary. I had a Vespa that I used to ride around on: I took pride in being someone who knew the working class neighbourhoods as well as, or better than, many of the people who lived there. As a student at the Liceo and then at the university, I went on exploration tours. I drove out to see the clusters of farmhouses, I discovered the huts where the gypsies lived. I recall that in the community we talked about the "new frontier", copying Kennedy. The new frontier was, and had to become, these outskirts. Our objective was to shift the frontiers of the city and to end the exclusion of the poor, and to do this we had to become familiar with the outskirts.

As a concrete job, strictly voluntary and self-financed in its day-to-day expenses, we took children who had dropped out of school, after flunking several times; and we ran a school for them, a working-class school, or an after-school programme when they started to go back to their regular school. This allowed me to say that the main reason *we* were going to school was to be able to teach the children. At a certain point I thought I had to go and live in a hut. We had to share more, we were "too bourgeois". We had developed a reading of the working-class suburbs as a huge desert. This was a social, secular reading that stressed one of the features of the outskirts, their abandonment, isolation, inability to communicate, their lack of internal resources for getting out of their state of acute necessity. This was also a religious reading, the outskirts as a desert where the people of God was destined to hear the call, to make their way toward the Promised Land. We began to build communities on the outskirts of the city: their members were women (on whom marginalization weighed even more heavily than on men), workers, unemployed young people... We've collected the texts of some of our meetings in the '70s, with a preface by Cardinal Carlo Maria Martini who, between 1975 and 1979, took part in the life of these communities before being named Archbishop of Milan.

What did Cardinal Martini make of you?

Giovanni Valentini writes about it:[4] "When he was still the rector of the Biblical Institute, Martini met Father Paglia[5] one day and told him: 'I'd like to do something with the poor. They call me everywhere to talk about evangelization and advancing the cause of human beings, but that's not enough; you have to stand really close to the weak, to the people with no voice, to the last in line.' Then, evening after evening, Martini began to frequent the little church in Trastevere for common prayer. And he got to know that little group of ordinary people. Among his parishioners, Father Paglia takes care of an old man in the neighbourhood who lives all by himself in the Via Del Moro, suffering, badly off, helpless. So the rector of the Biblicum dresses in mufti and decides to help that poor man. He puts on a sweater, rolls up his sleeves, and applies some elbow grease: he washes the dishes, mops the floor, puts the room in order. While he does his chores around the house, he resigns himself to listening patiently to the man's tirades against the Church and priests, without replying and without revealing his identity. Now engaged in the community of Sant'Egidio, Martini participated along with the other faithful in preaching the Gospel to the 'distant ones' in the poor suburbs of Rome. For a long time he celebrated mass every Sunday in Alessandrina, in a former pizzeria transformed into an outpost of that missionary task force. 'As soon as he could', Father Paglia recalls, ' – and sometimes his time was very short – he would return to the neighbourhood to visit the sick, to meet with the old people. While he taught catechism in the one-time pizzeria, there was also room in it for his lectures: the biblical scholar, with a blackboard, taught those boys some rudiments of Hebrew.'

"What interested him in the experience of Sant'Egidio? 'It's the Church', he's written,[6] 'that is really starting out from scratch. It's the insistent inner question that comes from the depths of the heart: where is the Gospel lived most authentically today? What are the places, the situations, that can best reveal the evangelical richness that we find in the primitive Church, in the Acts of the Apostles? In these situations of poverty and the original Christian enthusiasm.' Martini writes: 'The attention paid to the people living in the working-class suburbs of Rome explains the discovery of the themes, images and sufferings typical of these kinds of places: the winter cold, so hard to fight off in the damp houses, the loneliness, the sickness, the situation of women.'"

So your horizon was the world of the working-class suburbs?

The Roman suburbs were a special world, where different kinds of migrants from southern Italy formed a unique human and social fabric. We had gotten on familiar terms with a world to which the Roman dailies gave only limited coverage. The reality was absolutely tragic. "It's a litany of afflictions", wrote Giovanni Berlinguer and Piero Della Seta, "so different from the images spread by the dark chronicle of prostitutes, thieves, and pimps. To be sure, such people exist; but they are surpassed by these obscure, obstinate, silent figures of peasants from Calabria, from the Abruzzi, and from Sicily who have kept their dialect and the flavour of their land..." The world of the outskirts and the hovels was the other Rome. But it had a lot of inhabitants. In the 1960s the number of people living in huts was reckoned at between 30,000 and 100,000. The population of the working-class suburbs and tenements on the outskirts of Rome fluctuated around 600,000. At any event, housing, schools, and sanitation were problems for countless people; but in the working-class suburbs they became gigantic problems, in that city thrown together from makeshift houses built without planning permits and huts dating from the fascist era. It was the world of the poor, and our little community increasingly bound itself up with them.

26

How did your nascent community put down roots in these suburbs?

In the beginning we shared the lives of the people to some extent and taught in school for the children. Later on we tackled the problem of their relations with faith. The Church was rather distant from that world. They kept the memory of faith and popular piety from their original environment. In many cases a client relationship was set up with church institutions from which people had asked for help or entertainment. But could we say that this was enough, that the poor were having the Gospel preached to them? We thought long and hard about this: the texts collected in *Vangelo in periferia* (*The Gospel on the Outskirts*) are the fruit of our confrontation with the problems and this commitment. We read the Gospel among the poor; each one of us commented on it with his or her experience. In a parallel fashion forms of solidarity developed among the families with regard to concrete problems such as housing or school.

Was yours the only group involved with this experience?

We surely weren't the only ones to share this sort of experience. In those years there was a whole movement attending to the problems of the periphery; it was widespread among Catholics, particularly the young. It was a movement that bore within itself, though not clearly developed, the need for a different Church, a Church with a presence among the poor, a Church *of* the poor. Trying to live this different, new relationship in a new way, and trying to build it up with intensity, since we felt personally responsible for it – there you have some of our major ideas from those days.

The horizon, as you describe it, was without a doubt mainly a Roman one. Who was with you back then?

It wasn't a large group, but this question of yours gives me a chance to say something worthwhile about territory we'll cover later on. All the experiences that I'm talking about wouldn't have been possible without interaction and exchange with many friends of Sant'Egidio and other people as well. Up until 1974 we had never thought about setting up a community outside Rome. We thought that we had to work for Rome, to stay in Rome. There was a clear-cut reason for this: we had the impression that Christians hadn't had any great success in changing their world, that sometimes they preferred to go somewhere else, that they were, in a sense, deserters. Even the missionary tradition, which has brought together a large part of the most generous Christian impulses, had concentrated on *elsewhere*, on faraway places. Today I might feel differently about that. The link between the close by and the far off strikes me as evident. But, as we saw it in the early '70s, the city had to be changed then and there.

People joined our group for many reasons: to socialize, to discuss politics, to find some distraction... For myself, I took it all very seriously, and it was that way for others too; but for many it was just a passing episode. It was a time when young people were very socially active, with a lot of ebb and flow. We were alone and responsible for ourselves. There wasn't a single priest with us. Some priest or other might cross our path, but the first one to join us came in 1972. He was Vincenzo Paglia, and his presence has played an important role. He was the assistant pastor in a parish on the outskirts, an intelligent young priest who asked himself many questions. He understood these young people who wanted to build a new way of living the Church.[7]

Among the forces that launched you, was Vatican II more important or the late-'60s counterculture?

In the beginning I didn't have any direct or deep awareness of all the conciliar documents. But, some twenty years ago, I read a passage in the Council's message to young people where I found what was motivating me then. It said: "We exhort you to open up your heart to the dimensions of the world, to hear the appeal of your brothers and sisters and ardently put your energies to work serving them". I think we were struck by much of the spirit of the Council. I say that retrospectively. In fact, when the life of the community just started out, the Council was an atmosphere, something more general, intersection and ideas rather than specific texts: the need to change, to reform, the Church of the poor, the primacy of the Word of God. The remark made by John XXIII on the eve of Vatican II often came back to our thoughts: "The Church presents itself the way it is and the way it wants to be, a Church for everyone, and particularly the poor." The first text we took over completely was undoubtedly *Dei Verbum*, because of its connection with our discovery of the Bible.

Being a historian no doubt helps you to grasp the meaning of the Council...

Only starting in 1975-76. That was when I got a clearer notion of what the Council was and when I first had a strong sense of being a son of the Council. Sant'Egidio is a reality born after the Council and from the Council. The Council is a mine. Today I am convinced that it's the compass for finding our way to the next millennium. Without Vatican II our Christianity might have become nationalistic and fundamentalist. Thirty years later, at the end of the century, one doesn't have the impression of being far from the Council. To be sure, the passions of those years are spent now. And both the fears and the certainties of that period seem old-fashioned to me now. But the Council isn't far away; it let us experience the transition to a new condition, to the world after 1989 and the fall of communism, without getting lost. I'm also convinced that it spared us many evils.

Did the charismatics influence your way of looking at community?

We have had practically no relations with the charismatics, nor have they had any direct influence on us. I remember a visit and a long conversation at Sant'Egidio with Cardinal Suenens. But not much else. Still, the discussion of prayer has no doubt given me food for thought. More to the point, it's true that I like to encounter other experiences.

I think that the great risk run by community experiences is sectarianism, which leads people to live closed up in themselves and to mistake themselves for the Messiah or to believe that they've been officially draped in the mantle of the Gospel... To avoid that, you have to get to know a wide gamut of experiences and enrich yourself with them. This is one more reason why the Church is beautiful. Father Yves Congar, who came many times to Sant'Egidio and with whom a mutual bond of spiritual brotherhood sprang up, taught us that.

How can you define the difference between the community of Sant'Egidio and a charismatic movement? On the basis of social commitment?

Yes, on the basis of social commitment, but also on prayer. Our prayer is closer to the *Lectio divina* (or reading of Scripture and other sacred texts). One possible risk for a movement is to become imprisoned in itself, in its own problems or the problems of the movement's key figures, its leaders and its president; then there are the material questions, changing headquarters, interpersonal relations. You could spend a whole lifetime building a community that lives – and works hard – while spinning around itself, for itself. That's the risk hanging over every community whether of lay people or religious. The same thing applies to individuals, families, and institutions, including Sant'Egidio. Social commitment is very important with us. Trying to respond to the challenges of the world obliges us to move out of ourselves. Here's the difficulty: *Gaudium et Spes* remains the great question, which is: how to live the joys, the hopes, and the agonies of our world? The agonies of other people call on us to leave the house we have so carefully built. Every community, like every group and every family, knows its internal, human problems – the sickness of one person or other, the discussions, the different positions taken. It's possible to devote your whole time to searching for internal mediations. But the joys, the hopes, the agonies of our world oblige us to leave behind our own internal, self-referential logic.

Have you developed links with other church organizations?

Yes, with many of those who are making progress with their experience of the Church in Italy and, to a degree, everywhere else. There are also many bonds of friendship and cooperation with religious, both men and women.

One expression of this closeness is the celebration that we organize in Holy Week at Santa Maria in Trastevere in memory of the martyrs of recent years. The last time there were a thousand religious on hand. It was impressive, not just as an image but as an experience and a very strong memory. There were so many people that some of them couldn't fit into the basilica and had to stay out in the piazza.

Two years ago, the general of the Jesuits, Father Kolvenbach, the general of the Franciscans, Father Schaluk, the master general of the Dominicans, Father Radcliff, the superior of the Sisters of the Sacred Heart, the superior of the White Fathers and the abbot primate of the Benedictines, sent us a letter of friendship and support: "Your existence", they said, "is for us a source of joy. We believe that you are one of the contemporary forms of that gospel dream that guided Dominic, Francis, and Ignatius." They added: "You have dared to struggle for peace... It's important for the Church to have people who have the courage to run risks, throwing themselves into new initiatives, even if these can sometimes be judged controversial. Perhaps you suffer sometimes from the feeling that your efforts have not been understood. Don't lose heart. You are a marvellous example of the diversity and richness of the charisms in the Church."

On May 25, 1995 these religious superiors wrote: "First of all, thanks for the many important evangelical initiatives that you have undertaken over the years of your history. You have lived out in a highly concrete fashion your desire to be near the poor and the marginalized persons of your cities. We have been deeply moved by the simple and brotherly style with which hundreds of people are fed every evening in Trastevere, and by your work with old people, foreigners, and victims of AIDS. Solidarity requires human warmth, but active organization too. Thanks for your prayer each evening, where so many young people, feeling quite at home, receive their spiritual nourishment from the Word of God. Many members of religious Orders join each evening in your vespers, because they find there a welcome, meditation, and friendship. Thanks for your peace initiatives. Wherever we go in our trips around the world, we meet violence, the tragedy of war, and the suffering of innocent people... It must have called for a great deal of courage for you to take so much to heart the problems of Mozambique. In many cases people will have thought that you were insane, but despite that you have had success. Now you have directed your attention to the complex reality of North Africa and in particular to the tragic situation in Algeria. All these initiatives have been born from the spirit of Assisi, where year after year, following the steps of John Paul II, you have continued to gather men and women of goodwill who desire peace. We thank you from the bottom of our heart."

This letter, which alludes to the peace initiatives in Mozambique and Algeria, was an important sign for us. In the great religious congregations we see reflected many problems of the world, the dramas and the expectations of distant countries, the questions of war and peace. Our friendship with men and women religious, from our first steps in Rome until today, has never stopped growing in this perspective of "opening wide" our hearts and understanding the world.

The Sant'Egidio centre is located in the Trastevere quarter. Was that a deliberate choice?

Up to now I've spoken about our work at the city's margins. The community lived for a number of years without Trastevere. But at a certain moment we felt the need to have a meeting point in the city, to bring together the people who are busy in the various parts of the poor suburbs. How did we get to Trastevere? Once it was a strategic quarter of ancient Rome. Located outside the walls, it was also the city's port, a feature that it retained till Rome became the capital of Italy (in 1871). Very much a "people's quarter", in Roman times it was inhabited by workers, artisans, and merchants, a majority of them "Orientals" (Greeks, Africans, Syrians, Egyptians, Jews). Philo of Alexandria writes that, "This vast district of Rome, on the other side of the Tiber... was occupied by the Jews. For the most part they were freedmen". These Jews were probably among the first to adhere to Christianity. The first Christian community in Trastevere seems to have gathered where the basilica of Santa Maria stands today. Back then it was a barracks for veterans. In this place, according to tradition, a fountain of oil gushed up in the year 38 BC to announce the birth of the Saviour. In 217 Callistus, a priest of Trastevere, was elected Pope. Even when he became Bishop of Rome, he didn't abandon the quarter, but founded the *titulus Calisti*, the house-church named for him (there were also other house churches).

In the course of the first millennium, the basilica of Santa Maria became one of the religious landmarks in the city. In the 7th century, one of the first groups of priests who lived in community installed themselves alongside the basilica. Among them was Pope Benedict III. At the beginning of the second millennium, a *trasteverino*, Innocent II, inspired by St Bernard, gave the basilica the form it has today. When St Francis of Assisi came to Rome, he generally stayed in this quarter, which was close to the leprosarium of the port. With the growth of the city and the extension of the walls, Trastevere has maintained its character. Until recently it remained a very much working-class and sometimes violent quarter (brawls were common). Pinelli, "the painter of Trastevere", gives some depictions of them. The feast of the people of Trastevere, the so-called "festa de Noiantri" (or "our own Festival") expresses a strong working-class identity. Only after the Second World War did an exodus of the *trasteverini* begin, with the restoration of ancient buildings and the arrival of a new population. Up to now that has been the history of the quarter. But at the beginning all this didn't have any special meaning for us.

We were looking for a place. They had sent us away from the university chapel; so we went to the Camaldolese monks of San Gregorio on the Celian hill, near the Palatine. Then we rented an apartment in the centre of Rome, but it was too small and too expensive. We were already present in ten neighbourhoods on the outskirts. In each one of them we had a basement rented, generally, from the Institute of Working-class Homes. Old people came there, but young people too, and we organized courses for them. As soon as Father Vincenzo Paglia arrived we also celebrated mass there. We thought we had to strengthen and reinforce the centre city-suburbs connection, which is the opposite of the fragmented, disunited city. And then – this wasn't a minor detail – we needed a residence. At first we thought of setting it up in

Primavalle, in the poor suburbs, but that didn't work out. One day we heard that in the centre of Rome there was an abandoned convent. It was government property, and we took it over. Five years later, in 1978 we got a formal lease on it. So we have been in Trastevere ever since September 1973.

Can you imagine the headquarters of the Sant'Egidio community outside Trastevere?

Yes, we have many places where the community lives outside this quarter. But our main office is in Trastevere. That's the reality.

Isn't there a spirit of Trastevere? Do you find elements there that are original by comparison with the rest of Rome? A famous journalist, Igor Man, has felicitously described Sant'Egidio as the UN of Trastevere...

As a matter of fact, the community of Sant'Egidio could easily be found outside of Trastevere. It's enough to go to Primavalle or Ostia to find that this is true: we have deep roots in the suburbs. Today, to speak only of Rome, there are more than twenty-five centres. But the little old monastery has become a point of synthesis, a characteristic element of the community. It looks out on the Piazza di Sant'Egidio, with its little church, which can't hold more than two-to-three hundred persons; and it has given its name to our community.

But why the name of Sant'Egidio?

It's the name of the church. The cult of St Egidius (St Giles) probably made its first appearance in Rome around the 10th century, with the building of a little church, put up there outside the Leonine walls, at the end of the Via Francigena, which was followed by the pilgrims coming from the North. In Trastevere the origins of Sant'Egidio are more recent. In 1601 a first group of Discalced Carmelite nuns was established in a house on the Via della Paglia, close to the church of San Lorenzo in Turribus. In 1610 a butcher named Lancellotto Agostini obtained the church from the chapter of Santa Maria in Trastevere. He then had it restored and dedicated it to St Egidius. It was at this time that the painting by Cristoforo Roncalli, known as Pomarancio, which hangs today in the left chapel of the church, was executed. In the same year of 1610 Paul V built the monastery where, with the profession of the first nuns, the cloister was established. In 1623 the present-day church dedicated to Saint Mary of Mount Carmel and St Egidius was erected. The Carmelite monastery occupied one side of the Piazza Sant'Egidio. In the wake of the suppression of religious institutions after the unification of Italy in 1870, it became government property. The nuns had to get used to occupying only the smallest part of it. And so it went on until the day, some years after the Council, when they decided to abandon the damp building, which had become particularly uncomfortable, since no repairs had ever been made.

The overwhelming majority of the members of our Roman community live in other parts of the city than Trastevere. But the headquarters have become a kind of place of synthesis and encounter for this archipelago of groups scattered throughout Rome.

At first Trastevere wasn't much more than a container for us. Then, bit by bit, a true fusion developed with the quarter. From a place of welcome it has become a place of life. Today we're deeply engaged in it. At first our scooters and Vespas were stolen; later when it was learned that they belonged to us, the people stopped robbing them and gave them back to us. It was Fellini's Trastevere. Today it's changed, and not just for us; the whole social scene has changed. Trastevere is no longer just the working-class quarter of bygone days.

With time, and to this day, the subject of Trastevere has become more important?

Trastevere is an old quarter, it's the ancient port district, the existential crossroads of Jews, Syrians, and foreigners. We used to say in jest that if you dug deep enough into the subsoil, you'd find the prison of St Paul. But this is an important place for the Christian memory of Rome; Santa Maria and San Calisto, two churches located very near one another, are part of the first Christian cult sites in pre-Constantinian Rome. The Jewish community moved across the Tiber (around 1200), but there are remains here of the ancient synagogue. I think that the uninterrupted presence of a Jewish community in Rome for more than two millennia, even in moments of bitter intolerance, has enormous importance. It's in the city's chromosomes. Even when Rome was a completely Catholic city under a theocratic regime, it always maintained a Jewish presence. And this goes back to before the Christian era. You could say that in the face of so much immigration, even in the last few decades, the true Romans are the Jews of Rome.

Especially in the last fifteen years there's been an osmosis with the district. We left Sant'Egidio more and more often. There's another church, the basilica of Santa Maria in Trastevere, bigger and more beautiful than Sant'Egidio, which we frequently use. We went down into the street, we organized demonstrations. For example, on the anniversary of October 16, 1943, the date of the Nazi deportation of the Jews of Rome, we organize every year, along with the city, a torchlight procession from Santa Maria to the Synagogue (just across the Tiber), between the two poles of Roman memory. Recently we've promoted another demonstration on the problems of racism, from the Campidoglio to the Synagogue and from there to Santa Maria in Trastevere.[8] As part of this experience we have urged Italy to hold a day of commemoration on the anniversary of the largest deportation of Italian Jews.

The Community of Sant'Egidio has opened in the heart of Trastevere a "people's table", a dining hall for the poor, in the same place that serves for meeting, assistance, and education. Have you been backed by a sort of village solidarity?

Trastevere was a working-class district. The presence of a Christian community creates a space for the poor. A Eucharistic table and dining hall tables for the poor: that's the Church. Trastevere has loved these things. The solidarity is in the community that has contributed to creating them. Today we're recognized, the people love us. They're generally happy with us, with our presence; we're practically a source of pride. The Christmas dinner in the Basilica is served on the restaurant tables of Trastevere. When we organized the Prayer for Peace here, the merchants said: "Hey, we have the world championship of religions!" It's true, this village atmosphere is bound up with the life of the community. But the village is lost in a city as large and confused as Rome.

As a community, you're active in the poor suburbs, which were a side-effect of the postwar economic miracle with no structure or memory. For you, doesn't it come down to doing in the suburbs what you succeeded in doing in Trastevere?

That's a question that I find very interesting. When we began to work in the huts, things were different. Nowadays in Rome the huts no longer exist. There are the homeless, but that's something else again. Most of the time, apart from the social factors, the source of this condition is complex histories, personal problems. And then drugs came along, and AIDS... New kinds of poverty have replaced the old kinds, or have been added on to them. Our places in the suburbs try to be places of solidarity open to everyone. They're generally inspired by a community of persons who live in the district or thereabouts. Other people come from outside to bring help. There's an effort to create a fabric of solidarity in which to engage the poor and marginalized. You mustn't lose sight of the fact that the community was born after the discovery of these suburbs, not before. This place represents the synthesis of many experiences.

Isn't that synthesis realized every evening, with the prayers?

Yes. In 1973, at Sant'Egidio, we began to pray together every evening. To this day the practice has never been interrupted.

Who comes to these 8:30 prayers? Do your neighbours in the district also take part?

The locals don't come very often; they're more spectators. At first they were indifferent; today they're sympathetic. The people who take part in the prayers come from all over the city and from outside. They're persons with ties to Sant'Egidio. Some of them come from around the neighbourhood, others from the farther outskirts. There are also religious, men and women, and priests, many of whom are foreigners passing through Rome, pilgrims. This church is full every evening. And it's no longer the only place in Rome where the community gathers in the evening to pray.

In 1973 we had a lively internal debate over whether we could pray in public. For us, up until then praying meant getting together in a room, opening the Bible, reading the psalms, always in a closed environment or in some half-deserted church, or early in the morning before going to school. It was the model of the Acts of the Apostles: I talk with everyone; but if I invite my friends, I don't immediately invite them to prayer, only for conversation and discussion. And so in 1973 we opened the church for the first time in our history. We hadn't been at Sant'Egidio very long. We opened the church and began

39

to experience prayer as a moment of meditation as well. It was important, because in that moment we went from being a community that was warm but to some extent closed (because when you first come into the world, you always arrive with the conviction that you're a little unique) to a language of welcome, of openness, to a community that becomes an opportunity for others too and that finds its paths crossed and itself questioned by others.

How did the transition occur to your work as a historian? Is there an existential link between this profession and the defence of the poor?

I've alluded to the monasticism of St Francis. I used to ask myself what a community should be, and that was when I came across the Rule of St Benedict and the witness of Francis of Assisi. I made a choice for a free, autonomous, evangelical community, and a community for the open roads, for the suburbs, like the one Francis had. While I was reading the Benedictine and Franciscan texts, in 1973, the problem of my degree came up. I was mostly studying law, in the Faculty of Jurisprudence; but I couldn't stand commercial or Roman law any more. At a certain point, after I discovered Benedict and Francis, I began to read books on church history; and that got me very involved and interested. I found a seminar, not in my faculty, but in Political Science, directed by Pietro Scoppola, on the history of Church-State relations, and I began to attend it. I passed the exams that same year, and I asked if I could prepare my thesis for graduation. But on what subject? I wanted to do it on Rome, on Ernesto Buonaiuti and Rome, because I felt that Buonaiuti had understood the connection between the world of the Church and the social life of the city. Scoppola disagreed and sent me off in the direction of Henri Maret. And so I began my study of Maret, a French bishop and theologian, a defender of the reconciliation between the Church, the modern world, and democracy. In 1848 he was an editor of *L'Ère Nouvelle* with Montalembert and Lacordaire, then an advisor to Napoleon III on policy towards the Church, and a theologian who attacked infallibility at the First Vatican Council.[9]

How can a historian come to the aid of the poor? Isn't there a contradiction between the discovery of the huts and the profession of the historian? Isn't it easier, more immediate, and more effective, if you want to help the poor, to become a doctor or lawyer, someone who can concretely apply himself to the service of the poor?

My reasons were personal. First of all, I had no taste for law. I took my degree with rather good grades in almost all subjects, but towards the end of my studies I found I didn't like law, I could hardly stand it. I probably had an subconscious fear that if I did well in it, I'd end up working in a world I disliked, the world of the courts and lawyers' offices. I wanted to hold on to my freedom to work for the community. I was looking for a job that would leave my intellectual freedom intact. In the end, along came history.

Up till now I've mentioned this community of young people, the discovery of the suburbs, the enthusiasm... That was more or less when I realized that our meetings were at times highly existential, even existentialist, psychological: "I'm sad like this, I'm sad because of that, I have such and such a problem". I remember a film from those years; it seems to me that the title was "Let the Boss Drop Dead, Everything's OK", by Godard, in which an actor says that you have to "move from existence to history". I was struck by that, because it summed up in a phrase what I was trying to do. You had to find the way. I thought that the Bible was a history. And I began to develop a passion for reading church history, to which I had been introduced by Congar's books. I went to meet Father Congar in Paris. He told me that you can't do theology without history, that you couldn't understand the present without history. He said that history isn't the *magistra vitae* (teacher of life), but that it certainly creates a profound sensitivity to reality: "Without history you find yourself like illiterates who can't read the present".

That's how I gradually discovered the importance of history for understanding the world and the Church, for finding your roots. We had an intense desire to change the world, without forgetting the Church. The Church itself is a reality based on memory and therefore on history. With that end in view it seemed to me that I had to study history. For example, the history of St Francis; why be satisfied with a sweetly sentimental St Francis, the almost Hollywood version that has come down to us, when the original Francis was very different? And then studying history, working at the university, were activities I liked. It seemed to be a free, secular profession. (I wouldn't have wanted to live in an ecclesiastical environment.) My idea was to move from existence to history. This wasn't just an aspiration to study history or to do historical research, things that need more time to mature. Rather, it represented, in a certain sense, the wish to abandon a certain kind of psychological, overly intimate world that threatened to leave all too deep a mark on a community of young people and many experiences of politics and the Church about the same time.

But can history help the poor?

I don't know. I thought I could do that with the community. And history helped me to live. In studying it I encountered the memory of the Church and of our little-big world.

By searching for the truth?

Yes. By searching for the truth or, more modestly, trying to restore reality and, at times, complexity, as opposed to manipulations and oversimplifications. At the age of twenty-three or twenty-four, I took history to be a means for demystification and liberation. History *is* liberating, even though in a highly concrete and limited sense.

History is liberating: that would seem to be addressed to well-educated people with no material worries. Can history be liberating for the poor?

I think that history, like every other activity, has to accept its role as liberator only in relative terms. I believe that the Gospel is liberating. Just as the doctor can free people from suffering, but he can't give them a new life, history can free people "a little", relatively, not absolutely. In any case everything is relative, and I feel this relativity keenly. I have a professional life that gives me satisfaction; still I think that my profession isn't my liberation. There's always something beyond. I don't want to turn the historian's work into an idol.

Perhaps because the rigorous historian can't idolize anything? History provides a relative vision of things, and hence it has to protect us from ideologies, from fanaticism.

That's true. I think of my experience in the 1970s, which were a time of powerful ideology, with a Marxist cultural hegemony. But even in the first days of Sant'Egidio, though we were rather radical, we never shared an ideological vision. This shows how much we distrusted ideology, the distrust expressed by the boy who said: "First of all you have to change human beings". Later everything grew and took shape, became more precisely delineated within me... History, as you've said, has taught me to distrust ideology, received ideas, oversimplifications, the *cliché* of those who for years have spoken in the name of the "working class". History has always given me a sense of complexity. Cardinal Martini has written about the community: "It immediately impressed me by its joining together a profound sense of prayer and Scripture

43

with an intelligent attention to the poorest of the poor and to difficult social situations. At a time when there was a trend towards either the politicization of religion (to the point of adopting revolutionary theories) or towards a concentration on spirituality, the path they followed struck me as responding to what many individuals – and I myself – were looking for: a mode of evangelical Christianity capable of engaging the sufferings of people."

In the entourage of Sant'Egidio there are a number of trained historians...

Only a few members of Sant'Egidio are historians. There are many social workers, nurses, doctors, teachers and others, but there's a certain taste for history even in those who aren't professional historians. Let's put it this way, less ideology and more history, that's the way. In the years of ideology, history was a great help to us. The Marxist interpretation seemed logical, and in some aspects it was. But not everything that's logical is real or free from contradictions. And when it claims to be just that, it can only be ideological. You can make a similar observation about the very existence of our community. A simple ideological position consists in saying that the local Church is the parish: there's a core of truth there, as in all oversimplifications. But while it emphasizes an aspect that perhaps had been too much bracketed, it ends up not being true; and it has some rather serious consequences. According to this vision, in fact, the communities, the associations, shouldn't exist unless they make up a parish. But if you look at history, the life of the confraternities, the religious orders, the lay organizations, you quickly realize that the reality of the Church is much more diversified, much more rich and complex. Not to mention the richness – at times chaotic for us "Latins" and Italians, who are used to local churches entirely made up of Catholics – of certain eastern Churches. It's this sense of complexity that gives freedom of action. And it's knowledge of history that gives the sense of this complexity.

NOTES

1   See C. Vallat, *Rome et ses borgate 1960-1980. Des marges urbaines à la ville diffuse* (Rome: École française de Rome, 1995); F. Ferrarotti, *Roma da capitale a periferia* (Rome-Bari, 1972); and G. Berlinguer and P. Della Seta, *Borgate di Roma* (Rome, 1976).

2   Valdo Vinay (1906-1990), a pastor of the Waldensian Church and a historian of the Protestant Reformation, popularized the thought of Karl Barth. He was a member of the Commission on Faith and Constitution in the World Council of Churches. As a journalist, he followed the Second Vatican Council, emphasizing its innovative aspects and ecumenical significance. After Vatican II he did a great deal of work in the Catholic world on ecumenical topics, but also as a preacher. The Community of Sant'Egidio has published some of his texts in Valdo Vinay, *Commento ai Vangeli* (Brescia, 1992).

3   Andrea Riccardi is the author of, among other publications, *Roma, "città sacra"? Dalla Conciliazione all'operazione Sturzo* (Milan, 1979). The book surveys the history of the Church in Rome in the period between fascism and the Republic. This is a work of historical research based on numerous archival sources, which examines the idea of the "sacred city", recognized by the concordat of 1929, amid the reality of city life. Is Rome a special city? On the ground one can see a strong conflict between the fascist project for the *Urbs* and that of the Church. With the fall of the Mussolini regime, Pius XII and the Church became the great point of reference, even on the civic level, for the population of Rome. The book also examines the postwar years, when the Church and the Christian Democratic party were strong in the city, but people noticed that in his last speech to the parish priests of Rome Pius XII spoke of the city "almost as if it were a missionary land".

4   G. Valentini, *Un certo Carlo Maria Martini, la rivoluzione del cardinale* (Milan, 1984) pp. 21-22.

5   Father Vincenzo Paglia, today pastor of Santa Maria in Trastevere, was at the time a young priest recently made rector of the church of Sant'Egidio and ecclesiastical assistant of the Community.

6   M. Garzonio, *Cardinale a Milano in un mondo che cambia* (Milan, 1985) p. 29.

7   Vincenzo Paglia is also a historian of the modern era, author of *La morte confortata. Riti della paura e mentalità religiosa nella Roma moderna* (Rome, 1982), and of *Storia dei poveri in Occidente* (Milan, 1994). His role in the history of the Community is also important at the level of prayer and the liturgy. In recent years he has become especially interested in the problems of the Balkans and the former Yugoslavia, weaving a network of relations between the religious world, in particular the Orthodox, and the world of politics. He was one of the three members of the Vatican delegation that went to Albania after the timid overtures of Ramiz Alia.

8   On October 16, 1943 the Germans rounded up and arrested 1022 Roman Jews in the Old Ghetto and the whole city. After demanding the payment of a ransom in gold from the Jewish community, they deported all the Jews they could find, making use of the lists of addresses drawn up by the fascist police and not destroyed after the fall of fascism. The Jews of Rome were gathered together in Trastevere in the former Military College. Of the 1022 deported to Auschwitz 839 were taken immediately to the gas chambers. The Roman Jews who had escaped the roundup went into hiding, especially in religious or Vatican institutions. This roundup is a wound for the city and for the Jewish community; and, in the opinion of Sant'Egidio, it deserves to be remembered, above all at a time when we are witnessing a rebirth of anti-Semitism. For this reason, every year the Jewish community and Sant'Egidio organize a memorial demonstration. See S. Coen, *16 ottobre 1943. La grande razzia degli ebrei di Roma* (Florence, 1993). On Jewish-Christian relations see A. Riccardi, "L'evoluzione dei rapporti ebraici-cristiani", in *Amicizia ebraico-cristiana*, January—June 1991, pp. 19-33.

9   Andrea Riccardi took his degree in jurisprudence in 1974 with a thesis on canon law, *Società civile e società religiosa in Henri Maret.* In 1976 he published a book devoted to Monsignor Maret and French Catholicism in the 19th century, *Neogallicanesimo e cattolicesimo borghese* (Bologna, 1976). He has also written many articles on 19th and 20th century French Catholicism.

CHAPTER TWO

The Transition to Lasting Community

Many communities might take this motto: "We'll grow old together". At Sant'Egidio, founded by young people, how have you assured a healthy generational mix?

Sant'Egidio was born as a part of the high school and university world. But, as you say, we've grown old together. Today the average age is sharply higher than it once was. In Rome the students who were older at the time of the community's founding are about forty-five, like me; but the majority are around thirty. In the meantime, especially in the suburbs, different communities have grown up where the ages are widely varied; and there's no lack of old people. Thus Sant'Egidio in Rome looks like a network of communities, with offices in the poor suburbs and evening prayer in three churches in the historic centre: Sant'Egidio, Trinità dei Pellegrini (the ancient church of hospitality for the pilgrims and of help for the poor, where the influence of Philip Neri is strongly felt), and San Bartolomeo on the Isola Tiberina, the island between Trastevere and the ancient ghetto (site of the tomb of St Adalbert, who preached the Gospel to the western Slavs).

But there are plenty of young people. They're very different from the ones we met in the '60s and '70s. In those years there was a strong demand among the young for social and political commitment. Today it's different. The ones under twenty aren't attracted by all that. What they want to hear about is, if anything, the interior life and religion. Twenty-five years ago it wasn't easy to talk to young people about faith or the Gospel. I don't say that things are better now, but I find that there are fewer prejudices, at least at the beginning.

Do young people have the same experience of Sant'Egidio that we did? There are different approaches: they get close, they work together, but I couldn't say that they're completely a part of the community. We think that after us, or further along the way – if they want it – they'll have to construct *their* way of being Sant'Egidio.

But some people think of Sant'Egidio as a young people's affair...

Most of the members are young adults who've already made their family and professional choices. Sant'Egidio was born as a youth movement among young people. Today, you might say, it's got deep roots in the real environment of "adults". The dialogue with the world of young people is no longer natural, immediate, "physiological", as it was in the beginning; still it's extremely important. There's a continuing exchange between the world of the young and the adult communities. It also happens that some friends or a famous person visiting Sant'Egidio will say: "I turn to you, young people". But such friendship or kindness obviously fails to notice the white hair and the bald heads out in the audience.

Does a community of adults call for a very different structure?

I think so. It's not a community of religious, it's not a group of monks and nuns. Everyone at Sant'Egidio carries out some professional activity and has his or her problems like any other lay person. The permanent, full-time staff are very few, just enough to maintain a minimal office. In reality we would greatly prefer not to have any. Adults, unlike younger people, have less time, but they offer more stability and solidity. The degree of concrete commitment in service to the poor performed by the community – the social work that we carry on together – varies a good deal, according to the individuals. Some work with great intensity. There's also the possibility of a less active participation: it's a question of personal choice but, above all, the concrete conditions of one's own life.

I have to say that there are many persons who even though they aren't members of the community collaborate and make important contributions, especially in social services. The number is growing, and to us it's really significant. Obviously we're very happy with them, both for the concrete help they give the poor and for the deep brotherhood that they make possible. Other persons attend the community's evening prayer, without necessarily participating in its activities: they consider it a moment of spiritual growth. Among them there are also many religious. In a word, apart from the community in the strict sense, there's a wider circle of persons who recognize one another in the sensitivity and social commitment of Sant'Egidio, or of friends, very close friends, who recognize one another and feel strengthened by sharing the spiritual journey of the community.

But is there an internal structure of Sant'Egidio? How does it work? Are there people in charge?

Sant'Egidio is located half-way between a family and a formal structure. I would say that you need a family spirit to guarantee the different services. But you also need some structure. Every four years we have elections for a council and a president.

What's the structure?

The structure of the community is provided for by statute, and we're recognized by the Holy See as an international public organization of lay people. The approval – in keeping with the New Code of Canon

Law – came from the Pontifical Council for the Laity. The Community of Sant'Egidio is also recognized by the Italian government and has legal standing. The Community, as a non-profit organization, gave rise to a non-governmental body that looks after projects of cooperation in international development, as in Central America, Albania, or Africa. For some time now it has operated a Foundation for Peace, promoted by the Community, which coordinates efforts in this field.

The statute provides that every four years an electoral assembly, comprising forty representatives chosen from the various communities, elects in its turn the president and council. Generally these are the most respected persons in the community.

Extracts from the Statute of the Community of Sant'Egidio Association

Art. 2 – The first goal of the Community of Sant'Egidio is evangelization, the "essential mission of the Church" (*Evangelii Nuntiandi*, 14). The Community realizes that the Word of Jesus, "I must bring the good news to the poor" (Lk 4:18), applies to its life. And it makes its own the thought of the Apostle Paul, "For if I preach the gospel, that gives me no ground for boasting. Woe to me if I do not preach the gospel!" (1 Cor 9:16). The Community lives this commitment of evangelization especially to those who are far away, so as to form with them a single family around the table of the Eucharist, in mutual charity and the Spirit of the Lord.

Art. 3 – Another particular goal of the Community of Sant'Egidio is the service of the poor. The Community, taught by Scripture, knows that God is the defender of the poor: "The hapless commits himself to thee; thou hast been the helper of the fatherless" (Ps 10:14). It's aware that in such persons the Lord Jesus is mysteriously present, as the Gospel according to Matthew teaches us in chapter 25. In evangelization, in service to the poor, the community "wants to be" – in accordance with the teaching of John XXIII – "the Church of everyone and particularly the poor".

The last time around, one of the members elected to the council was a non-Italian woman. There's also a general ecclesiastical assistant for the Community, appointed by the Pontifical Council for the Laity from a list of three priests submitted by the Community.

This Council is the body that orients the Community. Its members include the president and the ecclesiastical assistant. But there are also important internal connections, with responsibilities for a given sector, for example our social services, whether on the local or the general level. And there's a deeply rooted custom of having a periodic general consultation for certain activities or geographical areas, among all the persons involved in any given activity, whether it be the service to immigrants from the Third World or to old people. To cite one example, Sant'Egidio takes care of several thousand old people in Rome. This allows them to live in their own homes and to avoid institutionalization in a nursing or rest home when that isn't necessary. For us this is an important obligation, but such work requires its own particular structure. Hence we have persons who manage these services and a coordinating committee made up of various local people in charge. In general all the specific activities are guided by a coordinating committee. That's what we do with the dining hall for the poor, with the family houses for old people, with the homeless, with help for people suffering from AIDS, with the handicapped, and support for the mentally ill...

Who appoints the people in charge?

The names come from within the coordinating committees – in agreement, of course, with the president or the council. But as a general rule there's an interpenetration of the impulses from the rank and file, from the wishes they've expressed, with the role played by the coordinating committees, which in this case is very important. Every four years, as I said, there's an assembly to elect

51

the council and the president. But quite often even important decisions made by the council arise from suggestions or requests that come from elsewhere and, precisely because they're important, become a choice involving the entire community, through the council.

When exactly can someone be said to be a member of Sant'Egidio? Does it depend on a degree of commitment, or does one simply sign up?

If I want to be a member of Sant'Egidio, I find myself at home in a certain spirituality and I'm accepted by the others as such. Joining up is the result of two wills coming together. Whoever wants to come takes a step toward the community, which accepts him or her. Here we have the highly explicit expression of two wills coming together.

In the meantime you have to give fair consideration to the fact that we've got no walls between the inside and the outside.

There are people who are close to the community and very important to us, people bound up with Sant'Egidio, even though you couldn't say that they're *in* the community, but they participate in it. For example, Monsignor Pietro Rossano, the auxiliary bishop for culture in Rome – who was one of the pioneers in relations with the non-Christian religions after Vatican II[1] – and is now deceased: he did a lot of work with us for ecumenical dialogue. He often came to Sant'Egidio; he was a great friend, but not a member of the community. I would say the same for the Waldensian pastor, Valdo Vinay. He too is dead now, but he preached every Thursday evening at Sant'Egidio for more than ten years. For many members of the community he was like an elder brother. He would come to baptisms or weddings; you'd often meet him there. Still you can't say that he was a member of the community. In these two examples what we have are two rather special persons.

But the old or poor person whom we help, with whom

we've been friends in Trastevere or Primavalle for fifteen years, for whom the people from Sant'Egidio may be his or her only relatives (in the strong sense of the term), can't in conscience be excluded from membership in the community. This is true even though, obviously, the two wills I alluded to earlier are expressed in different ways. Naturally the type of participation at some moments in the life of the community, such as prayer, is itself somewhat special. This kind of language about friendship is very important to us. The frontiers of the community aren't rigid. To be sure, we have to know who has the key to our residences, who's in charge of organizing the dining hall, etc. And yet, I can't say that there really is a radical difference between the members and the non-members. "Friends" are an increasingly more important category, one that counts a great deal in the decisions we make. In organizing the Prayers for Peace there's now a confluence between the members of Sant'Egidio and the "others", if I can call them that. The Syrian-Orthodox patriarch of Aleppo, Gregorios, has a crucial role, and I could cite others, including Jews and Muslims. They're people who count in the life of Sant'Egidio, and that also means our decisions.

But mightn't that bring on the risk of a certain fluidity in the organization, which could affect the bearings of the Assembly?

There *is* fluidity. But essentially our "functioning," the "look" of the community, always rests on agreements, on harmony with the presidential council and its members, and on consensus. Clearly, if we have to speak in these terms, different moods and opinions – at times different sensibilities – do find expression. But it's a fact that we spend a lot of time discussing and explaining what we've done and why, what happened. It's very important. After the first Colloquy on Algeria, for example, we had several meetings of an assembly to which we presented the situation, the events, the leading players. This sort of thing is indispensable for getting everyone involved. In another area, after Easter we organized a liturgy for all the old people whom we attend to in Rome, or at least the ones who can move about by themselves or with help. There were around two thousand in attendance. But for the members of Sant'Egidio the participation isn't limited to those who take care of these old people. So I can say that the community has precise borders: I know the people who are part of it, because I've known them for fifteen or twenty years; I know their families. Or, rather, everyone no longer knows everyone else, especially in the last few years. But at the same time we function as a network, and there's a great deal of internal communication.

So it's a network based on meeting other people, common prayer, and participation, rather than on some legal basis. But the latter exists, because it'll be necessary, when you've been involved in so many fields, to have a legal configuration for the State. Isn't that so?

It's necessary to have it, vis-à-vis the State... and the Church. At a certain stage people have to know who we are. It's a question of responsibility. Anyone who wants to sign up comes; sooner or later he or she meets someone or other in charge, takes part in prayer. We see him or her, see them again, begin to consider them our friends. They can ask to help, can commit themselves to some initiative and take part in internal meetings. In this sense you can speak of fluidity.

Perhaps an example will help to clarify this way of doing things: it's the case of a priest who lives in San Salvador. At some point he became the secretary of Monsignor Romero, the Archbishop of San Salvador who was assassinated in 1980. We've known him only since shortly after the death of Romero. Every year he comes to Rome. For many years now we've had a community in El Salvador with a membership today of around one hundred people. He's helped us, but he's not in charge of this community; he's not part of it in the strict sense. Probably one of the ways that he's helped us most has been precisely by respecting the birth of a community of lay persons, with lay people in charge. Still we consider him a member of Sant'Egidio, even though he never formally signed up. Perhaps later on we'll prefer to be more structured, but we still have the possibility of being creative on this point. In the statute you'll find the notions of Public Association and Spiritual Fraternity. The latter represents the association of people close to Sant'Egidio. It's still a community, but a community that has spread out.

You've mentioned the foundation of a community in San Salvador. How does Sant'Egidio spread outside Rome, outside Italy or abroad?

We never thought of organizing an expansion or a branch of the community outside Rome and its suburbs. But in 1974 there was an epidemic of cholera in Naples. We figured that beyond the huts in the periphery of Rome lay the South. It was then that I discovered southern Italy in a more clear-cut fashion. We had worked to send some of us down to Naples to set up a community: that seemed the minimum necessary act of solidarity.

Still, this system, which could be defined as the "classic" method of foundation – with some members who go off and try to bring something new to birth – didn't convince us. We didn't want to create a big movement, send people all over, and become in a way a congregation like the religious orders. And then we weren't up to it. The members of the community are lay people; every one of them has his or her life, here in Rome. We can ask one member or another to lend a hand – even on a regular, consistent basis – for a specific action, but that's different. That's why all the other communities of Sant'Egidio have arisen out of the discovery of our activities in Rome on the part of groups or individuals who eventually wanted to create something like it somewhere else. They come to Sant'Egidio, they participate in the prayers, they meet members of the community. Some, especially if they stay for a while in Rome, to study, for example, recognize themselves in our spirit, and it's as if they had absorbed some of it. If people tell us that they want to do something similar where they live, we tell them: "Fine, do what you can". Perhaps they write us to say that they've set up a group of five persons who work with poor children, etc. Then, whenever possible, someone goes to revisit them, and we keep in touch. At a certain point, it can happen that the situation evolves in such a way that the group becomes and is "Sant'Egidio". This method of communication and spreading of the community has been the most common. Many other persons, however, come here; then they try various initiatives without managing to find themselves in those efforts. In any event they remain our friends. Some succeed. Then the more the community puts down roots and grows, the closer we are to them. Speaking of Italy, there are, among others, communities in Rome, Florence, Leghorn, Genoa, Novara, Turin, Milan, Parma, Trieste, Padua, Naples, Bari and Catania. In Europe there's a fine Belgian community in Antwerp; in Germany there's one in Würzburg and another in Mönchengladbach; and then there are also communities in Barcelona and Madrid, in Lisbon, Budapest, Dublin, a little one in Prague, one in Kiev and one in Moscow. And so a European network is taking shape. All of them, roughly speaking, have emerged in the way I described.

Do all these communities bear the name of Sant'Egidio?

Yes, we give them the name of Sant'Egidio.

It's a sort of trademark?

Yes, if you want to use that word. According to the statute, the community in question agrees to be called "Sant'Egidio". Then when it reaches a certain degree of stability, it asks for recognition from the bishop.

In Kiev and Moscow you find yourself in countries whose Christianity is expressed above all in the great Orthodox tradition. Is the formula there the same?

To tell you the truth, the communities have the same spirit, even if practically all the members are Orthodox. But they recognize themselves in the brotherhood of Sant'Egidio. Of course, they don't consult much with the local Catholic Churches, even though the bishops are equally informed about it. Finding oneself in the heart of the Orthodox world is a new experience for us and, at the same time, a very important one. It's no longer simply a question of some non-Catholic persons following the community... It's different: we're talking about communities formed in large part by Orthodox Christians. It's still too soon to judge the impact of this on the Russian-Ukrainian world, or on us... But it seems to me that they're experiencing, after the religious conversations between parent and child came to a halt (as generally happened in the USSR), a renewal of faith. Faith for them is becoming real and being rediscovered along the lines of Orthodox tradition. In our communities in Germany there are some Protestants, but the majority is Catholic. One could make many observations about these experiences and draw important lessons from them. But the discussion would take us too far afield. Perhaps some other time.

Is there a hierarchical bond between these various communities and Rome? In the case of Rome can one speak of a mother-community?

We simply say "the Rome Sant'Egidio". But some also call us the mother-community. There are some people in our internal organization who are assigned the job of following these communities more closely and intensely and of maintaining bonds with them. The interchange is easy and necessary.

Do you organize meetings, like assemblies of general "chapters"?

Yes, at Easter we meet in Rome with most of the European communities. We try to get the largest possible number of members to come. In all, we have about 13,000 persons, of whom 4-5,000 come. These meetings are fundamental for getting to know one another better and for establishing relationships of trust. You have to recall that between the community in Kiev and the one in Rome there's the difference – apart from many others – that you'll find between people who have twenty-five years of history behind them and those who have only five. There's the difference in age of the people in charge: forty-to-forty-five years old in Rome, about twenty in Kiev. You also have to consider the problem of the numerical weight of each: with a grand total of about 15,000 members world-wide, more than 10,000 are in Italy, with the majority of those in Rome; so Rome makes up around half of all the communities. For this reason you absolutely have to try to prevent the others, to whom we owe a deep respect, from feeling "suffocated" or irrelevant – something that they obviously aren't. Then there's the problem of what language to communicate in, of the "vehicular" language. What language should we speak among ourselves? In all our churches in Rome we have simultaneous translations. The vehicular language is Italian, with French and Portuguese for Africa, Spanish for Spain and Latin America. Russian and English are also spoken.

It seems to me that these questions of organization show how Sant'Egidio is introducing into the Roman church tradition, which has pretty much got used to a certain legalism and a predominantly hierarchical approach, a different culture, strongly based on collegiality and ecumenism. But, for all this, it strikes me that you haven't lost anything in the transmission of the essentials or even in a family atmosphere.

In point of fact, we belong to a generation that can allow itself to invent things or at least to try them out. There is, above all, this relationship of inner trust, a respect for the responsibilities each one undertakes. This has to be taken into account and at the same time it's an important "organizing" element. But personal responsibility remains an indispensable factor in relations with the poor, in every choice. That's how it is even if no activity is ever based on a single person, but on a group of persons who are responsible for it. It seems to me that we aren't the sort of people who tend to want to decide everything in a top-down manner. If that ever happens, it's always to some degree a weakening, a sign that we're getting rusty. Sant'Egidio is based on mutual trust and on freely accepted authority.

We've mentioned the spread of Sant'Egidio in Italy and elsewhere in Europe. But the rest of the world?

This fact, which is very important for us, is rather recent. It dates from the 1980s. Today there are fairly well articulated and structured communities in San Salvador, Guatemala, Mexico, Bolivia and Cuba; there's another in Argentina and one in New York. We also have a presence in Africa, in Cameroon, in Ivory Coast, in Guinea (Conakry), in Mozambique and in Indonesia.

In the case of Africa, it's often a matter of young people. They've come to know Sant'Egidio; and the contacts that grew out of that have had important results. Hence when Sant'Egidio sees the light of day in Africa, it's already very African.

Is a Community of Sant'Egidio in Africa very different from a European community?

Certainly. As I said, before all else it's African, formed exclusively by Africans who are in charge of their own operations. The bond with us is a strong one, but their responsibility is also great. Naturally we met some time ago with some of the leaders and other members of the African communities. It was crucial. They have their own special features. And then, they're young communities, compared with the Italian ones. I'm thinking, say, of the one in Tabou in Ivory Coast, which grew up around a school teacher named Georges. In that community half of the people are from Ivory Coast, and half are refugees from Liberia. This is a highly significant fact. They recently composed an ecumenical prayer on the welcoming of foreigners. They've had experience with serving the poor, on a small but relevant scale. I think of the schools run by our communities in Mozambique or Indonesia, which gather together Muslim and Christian children. I recall the work done in prisons by our community in Conakry, where they won the release of two prisoners through forgiveness by the offended party. It's important – and here I'm thinking of the community in Cameroon – to discover that there are people poorer than you are, people who need others, beyond your own clan or family.

We devoted the last meeting to an exchange of testimonies and reflections on the economic, political, and social situation in different parts of Africa. For us, as for them, there's a feeling of anguish over development that has been late in arriving, even after the various plans for structural adjustment of the economy and the government requested or imposed by the West have been put into place. Some Africans had believed in miracles. This anguish comes from a continent that has been cut loose and left to drift.

For Sant'Egidio the brotherhood with these African communities is vital. It's like an alliance between our world and theirs. Physical communion with these persons is transformed into a profound participation in their situation. Independently of Sant'Egidio, communion in the Churches and among the Churches represents one of the main links between the North and South of the world, the will not to have our destinies torn apart.

And in Latin America?

There are communities above all in Central America. Each one has its history, but the work for solidarity is a characteristic trait of all of them. Every year at Eastertide they hold a Central American assembly. There's also a beautiful community in Argentina and, far from these parts of the world, a little community in Indonesia that's in close contact with the poor, most of whom are Muslims.

The brotherhood among these little communities, rooted in the most disparate situations, constitutes an important dimension for Sant'Egidio. It creates a circuit of nearness between different worlds, and it shows how evangelical love ignores frontiers.

Among today's charismatic leaders is there anyone who strikes you as particularly relevant?

It's hard to say: I think of John Paul II. Also the Patriarch Bartholomew I of Constantinople is a person searching for a charismatic role beyond the divisions in the Orthodox Christian world. Our ties with him are very strong. Before his election, he had visited our community a number of times (once on the occasion of the Rome visit of his predecessor Dimitrios, who came to Santa Maria in Trastevere). After becoming patriarch he visited the Community of Sant'Egidio in Antwerp in 1995, and the one in Rome later in the same year. He presided over a prayer session at Santa Maria in Trastevere and made a stop at San Bartolomeo on the Isola Tiberina, to venerate the relics of the apostle, his namesake. He was one of the first public figures to propose the community as a candidate for the Nobel peace prize, and in Antwerp he said: "There is a history of friendship, rich in encounters and exchanges, with your community, that has its roots in Rome and in the Patriarchate of Constantinople, the new Rome. Your community is dear to me."

What was your first personal contact with John Paul II?

I had never met Paul VI. I understood that Pope above all through familiarity with his texts and analysis of his speeches. I studied his pontificate during the '80s. But for me personally during his pontificate he remained a distant figure. To understand this, perhaps it's necessary to say something about how we fit into the local Church of Rome. 1974 was an important year. At that time Cardinal Poletti was assigned the job (1973-1991) of getting Vatican II to Rome, that is, of organizing the reception of the Council in the capital itself. The atmosphere of the period, as you can imagine, was tense; because on the one hand there was a powerful challenge to the institution of the Church, but on the other hand there was also some conspicuous resistance to the Council, much quieter but no less robust. Poletti's successor after 1991 was Cardinal Ruini, who directed the diocesan Synod of Rome, which was preceded by a whole series of seminars on "listening to the city", trying to address the changes in the Church and the city.

In 1974 Cardinal Poletti had organized a conference on *The responsibility of Christians in response to expectations of charity and justice in the diocese of Rome*. This served as a model for all the conferences of the Italian Catholic Church. Up until then we had been a highly marginal entity. We had little to do with the institutions of the Church, but we felt that this conference was a big occasion. We believed in the conciliar dimension and we felt consulted because of the dynamics of the conference. Just the way they organized the event was very strange and quite special: all the Romans who wanted to could sign up, speak out, and be heard. It was a sort of popular assembly. This represented a great challenge in the Pope's diocese. It's been said that with this conference the Council arrived in Rome, and that's true. We were living in an atmosphere of enthusiasm; and everyone had the concrete impression of being the Church. We went there too, and many of us signed up. We explained what the Community of Sant'Egidio was. We prepared a document calling for a special connection with the poor and proposing it to the congregations of religious present in Rome. Many supported it, both ordinary religious and superiors. There was the so-called "Letter of 149 Religious", which contained a rather radical proposal, but it wasn't "against", it was "within". It was an important experience of the Church.

Under these circumstances we chose our name. Before this we used to call ourselves "the Community". But, on the eve of this conference, we were all but forced to ask ourselves: "How will we present ourselves to the others?" We had discussions until late into the night; finally we opted for "Sant'Egidio", from the name of the place where we had settled.[2]

On this occasion the vicar of Rome got better acquainted with us. Then Cardinal Poletti came to visit us again. But the Pope, the curia, all that, had the air of being much farther away. Then there was the death of Paul VI, the conclave, and the election of John Paul I. Then came John Paul II, who begin to visit all the parishes in the city. On his first visit he went to the parish of Garbatella, a district in the old outskirts of Rome.

Why, didn't Paul VI visit the parishes?

Yes, he did a little, but not the way John Paul II has done.
The first parish John Paul II visited was San Francisco Saverio in Garbatella, where we have a small day nursery. We had opened it precisely in that district because a

baby had been bitten by rats during the night in an unsanitary house. Many of our activities got started, and still do, in similar fashion.

The Pope toured the parish and went to visit a convent of Capuchin nuns near there. As he passed by the windows of our day care centre, we called out to him: "Holy Father, come in, enter here!" He had the car stopped, got out and came in. We still have pictures of the Pope sitting on a very small bench in this rather bare place, joking with us. He began to question us, to ask who we were. When he heard the name Sant'Egidio, he couldn't help mentioning that in Cracow too there's a church with the same name. We explained to him a little about what we did and who we were; and he encouraged us: "You're in Rome. So come and see me!" It was our first meeting with him. We were impressed that the Pope should come that way, so simply. It was December 3, 1978.

Can you say that it was the first time that the Pope for you was really the Bishop of Rome, your bishop?

Yes, in our eyes Paul VI didn't exactly fit the description of our bishop; our bishop was in reality more concretely the cardinal vicar. By contrast, John Paul II has taken the situation more directly in hand. A few months later – in other words, very soon – he received all the associations of lay people in Rome. For the first time, we, the members of an "irregular" association, were admitted along with the "regular" ones. The Pope greeted these associations, walking from group to group. When he saw us, he exclaimed, "You! I already met you, I saw you in Garbatella!" This sort of thing might seem ordinary today, but it wasn't back then. Then came his visit to Sant'Egidio. He was supposed to come to the basilica of Santa Maria in Trastevere, which then had an old pastor; and the church, that gorgeous and rather large basilica, was half-empty. The Pope had told us that whenever we needed we could contact his secretary. Which is what we

64

did, suggesting that he make use of his coming to Trastevere to visit Sant'Egidio. The answer was: "Why not?" When the day came, he made his visit to Santa Maria in Trastevere. We were waiting for him at our church in the former convent, which was jam-packed, overflowing. Out on the street and in the piazza those who couldn't get in were crowded together. The Pope left the basilica and came to our house: he visited the whole place, he went down into the basement, parts of which we had already cleared. "But you have catacombs here!" was his reaction. His remarks were spontaneous, things like, "You're young, you've got the power of enthusiasm". The church officials on hand were rather scandalized and worried: in fact it was the Pope himself who walked, so to speak, into "the lions' den". And, after all, if the Pope comes to see you, that means you've been recognized as a subject of the Church: it's old Roman logic. That was how a friendship, rather than a recognition, was formed. It's something more.

Another time, during the summer – it was the first summer of his pontificate – a telephone call came with the proposal to go one evening to Castel Gandolfo to meet the Pope. Obviously we were glad to accept. In the garden, that July 22, 1979, there were around four hundred people from the community. I recall that until the moment I became a professor at the university, like others among us, I never wore a tie. And so we posed for pictures without a tie. Myself, Father Vincenzo Paglia, and another man, we went to meet the Pope in the palazzo; and we walked down into the gardens talking in different ways about consumer civilization. I recall several remarks of the Pope that struck me: "Look, I can surely say by now that I've got the antibodies to communism inside me. But when I think of consumer society, with all its tragedies, I wonder which of the two systems is better."

Those words, I have to say, opened up my geopolitical horizon.

Today the remark might sound banal, but then it helped me to understand the Pope's perspective better. On the same occasion we decided to speak to the Pope about the problem of Rome: the city, life in the city, how people live in Rome, what it means to be a Christian, the problems of young people, the poor suburbs. John Paul gave a very good speech and confided in us: "Through you, I know my Church, my Roman Church."

In his talk to us he also said: "The first idea is that of the spouse. The bishop has to be the husband of the local Church. The husband must reveal himself through words and deeds, and make people understand his love for his bride, both the visible love and the love that is within. At fifty-eight, after having been the husband of a Church for fifteen years I've been called by the Lord to be the husband of Rome, this most beautiful bride that is the Church of Rome. I'm trying to show through words and gestures that I intend to be a faithful husband. The first way that I took was the visit to the parishes. I believe that the parish visits have to be made, but I'm convinced that I must look for still other methods really to get to know my new bride – the Church of Rome."

In short, right from the beginning our rapport with the Pope developed under the banner of Rome. He was the Bishop of Rome. Then the relationship was continued through a series of meetings at Castel Gandolfo, and we spent feastdays together. Then there were also personal get-togethers. Once or twice a year I go with Father Vincenzo to have lunch or dinner with the Pope. And to talk about the most important questions, not only concerning the community, but the world, life...

The Pope returned to Sant'Egidio on October 4, 1993, for the 25th anniversary of the community, which was celebrated at Santa Maria in Trastevere. On that day he evoked our twenty-five year history as an "opening to the love of God, of commitment to peace, and of joyous response to the call to work in his vineyard". He added: "From the first steps of your community, by taking seriously the invitation of the Gospel, you have not closed your heart to the pain of the poor and have begun to think of your life as a debt of love and a permanent commitment to bear fruit. I recall what I told you when I visited you in April 1980: "Faith has to be realistic, because nothing of what is real is outside God, outside faith." Then he said again: "The passionate encounter with reality..."

Address of John Paul II to the community of Sant'Egidio during a meeting at Castel Gandolfo on July 20, 1980:

"We had already met a year ago for the first time. Back then perhaps you were fewer in number than you are today. You told me about yourselves with your songs, dances, and testimonies. Later we met on various other occasions, especially during my visits to the parishes of Rome where you carry out your mission, your apostolate. So I have been able to get to know you more closely in the working-class suburbs of Rome and in the parishes. Finally we had a meeting, let's call it the key meeting, at Sant'Egidio. It had been planned for March 9, a highly significant day for the parish of Santa Maria in Trastevere, because it was the feast of Saint Frances of Rome, a parishioner from Trastevere. But it wasn't possible to meet that day because I was slightly unwell. So the visit was put off till the last Sunday in April. And after visiting the basilica I was able to have the unique experience of meeting you at Sant'Egidio. I found myself among groups of workers and students, among old people, priests, even various generals of religious orders, rectors and superiors of Roman colleges; and I immediately realized that the community of Sant'Egidio is not 'homogeneous' but 'pluralistic', that is, a diversified community; and I believe that this is wonderful in that you welcome different persons, young and old. I wish to give special stress to this splendid feature: the sharing of your young life with that of old people. You make them young; and I must say that this has been a very successful experiment, because the old people among you seem even younger than the young ones. In following you I am trying to learn the formula, the principle of your community, of your activity, of your apostolate. After our repeated encounters I can tell you today that I have found this formula and I can begin to express it a little bit better than I could a year and a few months ago.

"You have the awareness that human beings, young, mature, adult, or old, both men and women, suffer for different reasons. There are external reasons, such as social conditions, politics, and the threats that weigh on the world. But they also suffer interiorly, in their heart of hearts, because of a kind of resignation, because they lack meaning in their lives. You have found the road, a very simple and purely evangelical road, to overcoming this resignation to the lack of a central point of reference for human life. You have understood that it's necessary to look for another human being, to find a community that gives hope and solidarity, two words that seem rather important for your spirituality, for your life and even for your songs... Hope and solidarity, if you will, are two very similar words: men and women are called to find themselves by means of communion with others, by means of solidarity with others.

"You have found this formula, which is the oldest of all: we see it already in the Book of Genesis, in the first chapters, which I have been concerned with for so many weeks now. On this formula you have shaped your experience of life, lived by different people, in different environments, here in Rome and outside Rome. And you have sought other roads beyond Italy as well, because your experience has proved interesting for others too, for other Churches, for bishops and priests, and for the laity.

"It's a very simple, very evangelical, very human formula. After a year of meetings with you, under different circumstances, and also after seeing that short film about your concrete experiences, I realized that this formula is the principle, the foundation of your community. And it's a very effective and profound formula, precisely because it's evangelical, simple, and human.

"You are surely capable of breaking through the isolation, the self-destruction of so many young people and so many old people. Among the young this self-destruction manifests itself in drug-addiction. You know how, and you have proved your ability, to overcome this self-destruction, because you have discovered solidarity with other people; and with them you have looked for solidarity or rather union with the Lord, with the Word of God, simply with God. You live out human communion in the same dimension brought by Christ, who has given us the greatest of all possibilities – of living human life, personal and community life, in the dimension of communion with God. This is what the Gospels propose. And when this proposal is made a formula for life, one has conquered for oneself and for others. Thus one becomes a true Christian, aware of the reasons for one's own Christian essence; and one also becomes an apostle, because the second flows from the first. As Bishop of Rome I must say that after a year of encounters with your experience, I am very happy to have you here in Rome; because I think that your movement, your experience, and your reality, everything that comes under the heading of the 'Community of Sant'Egidio', constitutes a certain evangelical leaven, which must increase the mass of this reality called the Church of Rome or, purely and simply, Rome."

I have never boasted about having the Pope's friendship or about eating with him, because it's something very personal: if *L'Osservatore Romano* announces the visit, that confers official status on it; the visit is a public fact. But otherwise I tell only my friends, which makes it a personal event and certainly not a claim to legitimacy. When someone tells me that so-and-so has been invited to dine with the Pope and that this is a sign of the favour he or she enjoys, I get very annoyed: because that's a way of using one's connection with the Pope to gain legitimacy.

Another important element to explain the relationship that has grown up between Sant'Egidio and John Paul II is the openness of the community to the problems of the world, an openness that the Pope has followed at very close quarters. I'm talking about the contacts made in El Salvador, in Mozambique, in the Arab world. Here in Rome we meet the Pope, who, precisely as the Bishop of Rome, performs a service for the Universal Church. And in this sense too his ministry has a special meaning for us. There's evidence of this in the talk he gave to the community on February 6, 1988, when he received our members at the Vatican: "I remember the many meetings I have had with the Community. In the beginning of my years as the Bishop of Rome, while visiting Garbatella – it was in December, 1978 – I came across your charity work and visited the site. After that first time, I have often met you in the outskirts of the diocese, during my visits to the parishes, but also in the church of Sant'Egidio and at Castel Gandolfo. And then I found you elsewhere in Italy and in various parts of the world. I have had many occasions, down through these ten years, of following you and listening to you. This has been for you a period of internal growth and of development outside of Rome as well, during which – on Pentecost, 1986 – you were recognized as a Public Association of lay people by the Holy See.

"It's no accident that for your twentieth anniversary you have gathered in Rome and come to pay a visit to the Pope, who is bishop of this Church. Your Community was born here, in 1968, from a group of students; it has grown up in this Church of Rome 'which presides in charity'. Then you spread elsewhere, engaging yourselves in other local Churches, but still maintaining a strong sense of the 'Romanness' of your origin. I told you at Gastel Gandolfo in 1986: 'Wherever the Communities of Sant'Egidio are – even when they're not in Rome –

they are always Roman'. This character doesn't seek to be a reason for pride or privilege. What finds expression in it is rather the primacy of charity that Jesus inculcates so insistently in the Gospels: 'Whoever would be first among you must be the slave of all' (Mk 10:44). The Community of Sant'Egidio has lived this service, according to its Statute, in evangelization, in the choice on behalf of the poor, in friendship and hospitality in an ecumenical spirit of dialogue.

"Evangelization has given rise to your Communities in various countries of Europe and Latin America. Right from the beginning you have heard the words of the apostle Paul to the Corinthians: 'Woe to me if I do not preach the gospel'. But he adds: 'What then is my reward? Just this: that in my preaching I may make the Gospel free of charge...' (1 Cor 9:16.18). And, seeing the fruits of the Gospel, I am glad to rejoice with you.

"Whomever you meet you teach to love the poor... This is a basic aspect of the formation you give young people: love for the poor. Continue to orient them to this daily commitment in life. Those who are in trouble must be able to find help with the Communities of Sant'Egidio..."

John Paul II underlines the importance of the reception given to old people and foreigners, and he welcomes the promotion of interreligious dialogue. He adds: "The primacy of charity, the wellspring of evangelization, of service to the poor, of all dialogue, is the heart of your work. It is also a legacy of the Church of Rome, which you have rejuvenated. To strengthen yourselves in this you lean on Christ through prayer. I am happy to know that you are persevering in daily prayer in the evenings, in the church of Sant'Egidio and in many places in Rome and elsewhere. On this twentieth anniversary I would like to remind you that the secret of your commitment in all directions is here: it is in Christ who, in prayer and love, manifests himself as the 'foundation' (1 Cor 3:10) of everything we build."

In a word, more than anything else we have had a relationship characteristic of young people who spoke frankly to him about many things. I think that this amused him a little and that he was happy with it. He's always been affectionate with us. It wasn't as if he were our protector. As a bishop he's concerned about regulating as best he can the ecclesial situation of Sant'Egidio. For Trastevere he wanted the parish to be served by priests from Sant'Egidio. It's been an intelligent choice, because without this the district would have had a weak parish and a strong community. And at the same time he's given vitality to a great basilica that was at risk of languishing.

John Paul II to the community on February 6, 1988:

"This sense of hospitality and universal brotherhood is also found in the commitment to ecumenism and dialogue that Sant'Egidio lives by participating in the vocation of the Church of Rome in its local and universal dimension. Your community, which was originally so small, has placed no limits on itself except those of charity."

Isn't there another point in common between John Paul II and Sant'Egidio: Assisi?

Yes, there's also the adventure of Assisi. We felt the Assisi prayer for Peace intensely, and we've tried to continue it.[3] At the time practically everyone was opposed to repeating the Prayer for Peace and the encounter between the major world religions. Even the cardinals who had been most involved in it maintained that "Assisi" was the Pope's thing and, in any event, unrepeatable. Then, one year later in 1987, we invited some religious leaders, and leaders, and we carried out the prayer, in Trastevere, in the piazza of Santa Maria. We asked the Pope to receive us; there were bishops, muftis, rabbis. John Paul II read a speech, then he came toward me, calling out, "Professor, you almost got excommunicated!" I was worried and didn't know how to respond: "Holy Father, if you say so..." But the Pope had grasped what was going on and took back the microphone to say: "Be brave, Assisi has to be continued". John Paul II has always played the part of encourager. He has never overdramatized the problems. Still, he's not the one to resolve the possible difficulties with church structures. You have to talk, explain and discuss things with the people directly concerned.

The Pope has a sense of pastoral relationships, he encourages the initiatives that seem good to him. This has been very important for us. In my view, he's a great figure, and I don't say this just as an historian. In the experience of our community he's a great personage, a source of encouragement.

But you see him as a bishop. This seems to be a major point with you.

Yes, it's a deeply rooted idea.

He's the bishop of your diocese who – if I understand you rightly – becomes Pope only in a second stage of your relationship.

In the beginning for some people the connection we established with the Pope meant something like, "You've made a choice in favour of power". In reality it was something altogether different for us: he was our bishop. As I see it, you have to leave behind the logic of the sovereign to whom I betake myself because I need an appointment or some pleasure, or because I want to speak ill of someone and get him condemned. Obviously the Pope is an influential man; we're not children, and we know this well, but for me he remains a bishop rather than a sovereign.

But at this stage of our reflections isn't there a contradiction, or at least a difficulty in the relationship with the bishop-Pope, since he presides over an administration, the Roman curia? You may see him primarily as the bishop, but the curia sees only the Pope. In other words, is it possible to set up balanced relations with the Bishop of Rome and with the Pope?

I'd like to make it clear that the Pope is the Bishop of Rome, but that in Rome there's another person who plays a decisive role in the pastoral life of the diocese: the cardinal vicar, who is, despite the second half of his title, a permanent official. He's the one who presides over the life of the diocese. In Rome the whole world of the diocese, with its curia, its auxiliary bishops, and its parishes, revolves around the cardinal vicar. Rome is a diocese like any other. That's what Paul VI wanted with his diocesan reform. Before that, the situation was different: the influences on religious life were many, and there were some exemptions from the vicar's authority. Despite this normal "structuralization" around the vicar, the Pope always remains the real Bishop of Rome. That's how John Paul II wants it. One time in Holland I had gone to talk about Sant'Egidio, and someone said to me: "I'm amazed to see how you manage to be free in Babylon!" For the people I was talking to, Babylon meant the Rome of the curia. I am aware, since I studied it as a historian, of how complex the curia is, of the tendencies that run through it, of its moods, of the problems of who's in charge of what. There's a real historical difficulty here, and it's hard to get rid of it with a couple of wisecracks.[4]

So long as Sant'Egidio remains focussed on the problems of the city, you don't necessarily have to run up against the curia. But that's not how it is when your concerns become worldwide and a relationship with the Secretariat of State becomes, I would think, indispensable.

In my view one has to be careful not to "use" the Pope as a means of evasion. Another risk is to say to yourself: "The Pope supports us, so..." The Pope can't be used to legitimize our initiatives or anyone else's, just like that. The history of religion teaches us that in certain countries Catholics made war on each other, with each side in turn calling on Rome to be its witness. But the curia takes the part of the Church of Rome. On account of this, for some years now we have had connections with many people, which doesn't mean that we run an organic network or a lobby. Nor does it mean the opposite, just casual connections. But it seems impossible to me to build up something that's *de facto* a part of the Church in Rome without connections with the people who work for the Church Universal. To be sure, the question is, what kind of connections?

I very much want to be precise on this point. Do some people like to come to Sant'Egidio to pray? Good. Do others like to come to talk? Good. Do they want to have us share their experiences? That enriches us. They don't mind listening to us, eating with us? I think of the meetings of St Philip Neri and the church historian Baronius; the Oratory was conceived somewhat along these lines. There was this person and that person, and others also, who came to visit. That's been our experience: the contacts enrich us. Common prayer and friendship are normal in a local Church, even if it's a special case like Rome. I might consider some of the people in the curia my very close friends, but I'm conscious that Sant'Egidio is a controversial subject. You have to accept the evidence: everything is discussed or discussible. We're not the Messiah, that everyone should have to identify with us. I don't like the mentality of certain groups that think themselves messianic; it bothers me. Some people measure the "holiness" of others according to the degree of identity they achieve in their relationships with them. But history is more complex. And the Church is large. At the same time I think one shouldn't have a curial policy and, certainly, that's not our role. We're a reality of the Church; we have demands, ideas, experiences.

For example, I know that on the issue of Algeria some people in the Church are opposed to us. I know this very well. And still, why disapprove of us? Aren't we Catholics too? Don't we pray? Our efforts on behalf of Algeria are a service that we've chosen to offer, without the slightest admixture of anything else. I have my convictions, which not everyone shares; but nobody can doubt my good faith and my Catholicity. It's hard to say who's right in such a controversial situation. We'll see, later on, who *was* right; that's all I can say today.

But I think that offering a live ecclesial reality, based on the poor, on prayer, on openness to the world, also means bearing a humble witness in Rome.

So you don't ask John Paul II for his personal protection?

No, the Pope expresses his sympathy, which is very paternal, with regard to us. We're content with that, and we welcome it with joy; but we know that there's a responsibility incumbent on us that can't be anyone else's.

Can it happen, above all on a delicate issue like Algeria, that communications or letters come to the Secretariat of State aimed at blocking or interrupting your action, and that the Secretariat of State might put the brakes on you?

Yes. But I also think that it's not right to use the Pope as a shield. Let me explain: there's the bishop of Rome, who is a father and a friend; and there's the Pope, the head of the Church with all his responsibilities.

76

Could the Vatican ask Sant'Egidio to make contacts, to organize delicate meetings, for which, perhaps, it couldn't directly take the initiative itself?

Yes, certainly; but that's never happened, even though the newspapers sometimes write that we're the Vatican's "parallel diplomacy". There's no offence in saying that, it's just not true. In reality your question raises the problem of the Pope's will. We owe obedience to the Bishop of Rome, the minister of the unity of the Universal Church – that much is clear. Does it mean that with every initiative we have to come to an agreement with some office of the Holy See or request prior authorization? We believe we have to decide freely and responsibly, but we also have to inform the Vatican about our activities. For us it's a fundamental principle: provide information, and provide it first, don't come up with a *fait accompli*. But neither do we ask for an authorization that, whatever the answer might be, would serve as a cover and so free us from the burden of responsibility. We consider this the key to fraternal relations. To each one his or her responsibilities. When one of our initiatives has diplomatic implications, we inform the Italian Ministry of Foreign Affairs; that way the news gets around, and there's an awareness at the level of the European Union.

Take the example of the negotiations on Mozambique: the Vatican played no part in them. There was a Mozambican Archbishop in the mediation group, but the Vatican wasn't involved. Instead, the government of Italy acted quite directly. It seems to me that the Vatican has a greater tendency not to want to "hide" behind an independent initiative. I know that all this is hard to explain. Basically our experience is that of the dogma of Chalcedon: no confusion of realms, but at the same time no separation. We can't establish separation: we're in Rome, we live here, we're part of the human and religious fabric of Rome, but we're not confused with Rome. So there's no confusion of who's who or who's responsible for what... You have to have a concrete idea of this Rome, where the division of responsibilities is clear, and where there's a fabric of common life and a dialogue that's quite as lively and concrete.

NOTES

1 Pietro Rossano, a Piedmontese, born in 1923. After studying at the Biblical Institute, he entered the Curia. As secretary for the Secretariat for non-Christians, he took many trips, establishing important relations with representatives of Islam and Oriental religions. The reception of *Nostra Aetate* was at the centre of his work with Cardinal Pignedoli. In 1982 he was named rector of the Lateran University and auxiliary Bishop of Rome for culture. A collaborator with Paul VI on ecumenical dialogue and with John Paul II on the problems of Islam and culture, he died in 1991. A man of dialogue, he wrote: "Dialogue will not be really possible unless the interlocutors know one another... And real knowledge of the other cannot happen without respect, sympathy and friendly association." Cf. *Il dialogo non finisce. Pietro Rossano e le religioni non cristiane*, texts collected by the Community of Sant'Egidio (Brescia, 1994).

2 Sant'Egidio, in English St Giles. His tomb is located at Saint-Gilles-du-Gard, where he supposedly lived as a hermit. He is said to have been born of a noble family in Athens in the 6th century. A miracle-worker from his youth (he cured a sick man by covering him with his cloak), he went to France to live as a hermit (he is believed to have gone to the school of Caesarius of Arles). In a forest he met the Visigoth king Wamba, from whom he protected a hunted doe (a symbol of his defence of the poor). The king had a monastery built for him that he donated to the Pope during a pilgrimage to Rome. In the wake of the Muslim invasion of France it was put under the protection of Charles Martel. A populous centre grew up around the abbey, and the cult of St Giles spread throughout the Middle Ages. Many churches were built in his honor, and Saint-Gilles became a stopping place on the pilgrimage to Santiago de Compostela. The downfall of his cult began with the struggle against the Albigensians; and the abbey was destroyed during the wars of religion between Catholics and Protestants. Cf. P.E. d'Everlange, *Histoire de Saint-Gilles* (Marseilles, 1980).

3 Community of Sant'Egidio – Uomini e Religioni series, *Mai più la guerra. War Never Again* (Brescia, 1990), and *Pace a Milano* (Cinisello Balsamo, 1993); see also the Community of Sant'Egidio, *Religion in dialogo per la pace* (Brescia, 1991).

4   A. Riccardi, *Il "Partito Romano" nel secondo dopoguerra (1945-1954)* (Brescia, 1983). This is a study of the church lobby around Cardinal Ottaviani, who, prompted by ecclesial motives and Italian politics, opposed Monsignor Montini. See also, ed. A. Riccardi, *Pio XII* (Bari, 1986) (a study of the Pacelli pontificate and its relationship to Italian Catholicism, and on the uncertain and complex identity of the Church in Italy). Among other works by A. Riccardi *Il potere del Papa da Pio XII a Giovanni Paolo II* (Bari, 1993) is notable for the fullness of its synthesis.

CHAPTER THREE

In the Struggle Against Poverty and the Battle for Peace

Is there a link between the defence of the poor and the defence of peace? Sant'Egidio's point of departure is located on the outskirts of Rome, where the children of the bourgeoisie discovered poverty. How do you go from working against poverty to defending peace? And when does one carry more weight than the other?

I'd like to start out with the last part of the question. When we got to the end of the negotiations on Mozambique, we were discovered by the international media. A journalist from the *Washington Post* asked me a question that went more or less like this: "When did you leave off your work of social solidarity to commit yourself to diplomatic action?" I replied that our work of solidarity isn't over, that it's still going on, that for us diplomacy is something unusual. Our daily life is with the poor. But I can add that there's no contradiction or difference between solidarity with the poor and solidarity with the poor nations. War is something like the mother of all forms of poverty. War makes everyone poor, even the rich.

It's the same culture of solidarity. How did our work for peace in Mozambique get started? We were collaborating in development with that country, but we knew that the cooperation was hollow, a mere palliative, without peace. Ultimately, working for peace was a form of cooperation, a way to develop the culture of solidarity. We discovered that friendship, solidarity, and faith in certain values constituted a force. But Sant'Egidio didn't become, for all this, a sort of Ministry of International Relations. During the two years of negotiations on Mozambique, prayers were held every evening at Sant'Egidio. Every evening at 8:30, as always, the bells rang out. All our activities went on as before. In brief, there's a strong culture of solidarity; the promotion of peace is an extension, an elaboration, of this. Furthermore, in helping the poor who are close to us we find many distant problems: the dialogue with Islam, for example with Muslim immigrants. The same thing happens with the problems of southern Italy.

Isn't there a problem of peace in the relations between the national community and the communities of the immigrants?

Sure. The problems in this area are extremely numerous, and they're on the increase. The 20th century Church has discovered that one of its principal missions is peace. In the Popes who have succeeded one another you can see a real growth of this awareness of peace. Christ sent his disciples to announce the Gospel and to heal diseases; but isn't war the most serious disease in this world? And isn't peace the greatest healing that Jesus' disciples can bring? Yes, it's the miracle of peace.

That's why I believe that on this point the Church mustn't limit itself to delegating everything to the Pope. He talks about peace, but no one pays attention to the opportunities that Christians can seize to get involved with it themselves. Besides, war grows out of the accumulation of violence. Shouldn't we be more demanding about living the words of the Gospel: "You have heard that it was said to the men of old, 'You shall not kill...' But I say to you that everyone who is angry with his brother shall be liable to judgement; whoever insults his brother shall be liable to the council" (Mt 5:21-22).

The Mozambique peace accord was signed on October 4, 1992 in Rome, at Sant'Egidio, after twenty-six months of negotiations. With the accord FRELIMO, the front in power from the year Mozambique won its independence (1975), came to terms with the guerrilla movement of the anti-Marxist opposition. The signing came about at the end of an unusual mediation process, led by Andrea Riccardi and Matteo Zuppi for the community of Sant'Egidio, by the Mozambican Archbishop Jaime Gonçalves, and by the deputy, former undersecretary of foreign affairs, Mario Raffaelli, representing the Italian government. Thanks to the patient work of establishing contacts on the part of Riccardi and Zuppi in the '80s, the warring parties came together in Rome.

In the course of the Roman negotiations at Sant'Egidio, the mediators created a synergy of forces, governmental and otherwise, using diplomatic-legal methods, but also a practical wisdom that led to the final success. In the last phase, observers from the UN, the USA, France, Great Britain, and Portugal were given accreditation. Patience and perseverance were the leitmotiv of the negotiations, which convinced the parties present to move step by step to an accord.

The "unlikely team of mediation peace-brokers", as described by the *Washington Post*, worked to soften men who had become hardened by more than ten years of war, but it also set up a technically complex peace process that concluded happily with the free elections of October, 1994. The United Nations Mozambique mission of 1993-1994, no doubt the greatest, if not the only effective, success of the UN in recent years, was carried out on the basis of the Rome accords.

The link that passes through everyday life is the connection between poverty and peace. As long as there is destitution, peace won't be guaranteed. This is what's affirmed by the solemn, inseparable pair, "justice and peace". I believe that in our world, which takes for granted the presence of broad stretches of poverty, situations full of tension and possible wars are building up. But violence and war aren't born only out of poverty. Wealth produces them too. We've also discovered that the commitment to peace is bound up with prayer. Peace constitutes one of the principal aspects of our community prayer, and this orientation has been encouraged by the visits here of many Christians from all over the world. Some of them talk to us about the painful conditions in their countries, devastated by war and poverty; and we can help by remembering them in our prayers.

The efforts for peace by a community like Sant'Egidio are timely, but how do you choose? Why Mozambique and not Angola, Algeria rather than the former Yugoslavia?

The choice is connected to history, to life; and it's not exclusive: there are meetings, possibilities, friendships... something of an inevitable destiny.

Can war be stopped?

It's the problem of prevention. It's not true that nations seek out war for war's sake. They fight because they don't see any other way. I stayed in contact with the Mozambican guerrillas for two and a half years. Why were they fighting? Because they saw no alternatives to combat. And they wound up getting used to it. But then, during the negotiations, I witnessed the evolution of the guerrilla, the transformation of the warrior into the politician. In my view this is already a great miracle; because I'm convinced that even if in principle no human being wants war, it's still extremely hard to find the path of mediation. It's difficult and exhausting to escape the logic of conflict and violence. Sometimes it's like a tunnel. We all experience some conflicts, every human community knows them: but how far should such conflicts be pressed? There's the problem. At bottom, the Mozambican guerrilla was waging war because he didn't believe that the conflict could be transposed, shifted, and translated into other categories more compatible with daily life. He didn't believe in the possibility of political struggle. The creation (or reconstruction) of *homo politicus*: that's the great problem of peace. To be sure, the protagonists don't necessarily have to reconcile, they can continue to hate each other, even for a long time; but having tense relations is one thing, shooting back and forth is another.

You've spoken of guerrillas who turn into politicians. But doesn't history offer many contrary examples, of men living a culture of war? Isn't there an instinct for war and aggression?

An instinct for struggle surely does exist. Still I think that there's not much use in philosophizing about it. The real problem is situating the question, reflecting on the individual cases, for example, that of the Algerian fundamentalists. I'm convinced that when you make war for years, it becomes a second nature, an instinct. As we were welcoming the Mozambican combatants here in the garden, a helicopter flew overhead. Nothing could be more normal for us, but they were terrorized by it. They were men who came from the bush; and the only thing they knew was how to make war, the weapon of the desperate. This is the first problem. There is, in addition, a will to war that – as you were saying – is present in some politicians. I've constantly observed it in the case of Mozambique. The ruling class set out a choice: win a military victory or else negotiate the surrender of the adversary. But the latter wasn't recognized as a conversation-partner. This is just one type of problem that emerges in the absence of a democratic culture, of a peace mentality. When does it happen that a country slips more easily into war? When it's totalitarian. We've had this

84

experience in Germany and Italy, which went to war without any trouble because they were ruled by totalitarian systems. People often talk about the spirit of Munich as a collapse of the French and the English in the face of Hitler's aggression. But there's another element to consider here. I surely don't want to justify Munich, that doesn't interest me. But it strikes me as opportune simply to underline the fact that every democracy hesitates to enter a war: think of the USA before the First and Second World Wars. Yes, I believe it's easy to agree that a democracy has a harder time going to war. Why? It's an interesting research topic. Democracy develops antibodies against war, while a totalitarian regime is more capable of signing a treaty today and declaring war tomorrow. Among the reasons this happens is that basically it's imbued with the culture of violence, force, and war. By contrast, democracies identify more readily with peace.

Can peace be protected by waging war?

That's the problem of governments. Each one has its own role. I don't do moral theology about war. I remain convinced that war is terrible and that its consequences weigh down on an entire generation and beyond. We know that well in Europe, where we weren't set free from the consequences of World War II until 1989. War is always a very serious choice, but is it really a choice? It's often a tragedy that brutally invades the life of a people. Characteristically it distorts the moral qualities (and that's not all) of entire nations. We mustn't forget the lesson of the Second World War. Even the years after 1989 have known a new euphoria of wartime violence. The history of the former Yugoslavia proves this. But violence isn't isolated there: it's diffused, spread all through Europe and the world. And now it has terrible weapons at its disposal. War – and what destructive capabilities it has! – remains the resource of the desperate and those living outside any international logic. In this sense war has taken a new turn after 1989, with the end of the Soviet-American confrontation.

The new situation also leads us to reflect on countries like Italy that, unlike France or Great Britain, have never thought seriously about the problem of providing themselves with a full military arsenal. The scenario is a new one and demands serious thought. Still the debate remains limited. There's little talk about the new nuclear dangers, which are much worse than in the past, with uncontrolled proliferation, the very worst kind of smuggling, of atomic weapons. And is the nuclear potential of the East under control? It seems to me that people today remain too removed from these serious problems, which concern all of us. This – along with the concealment of international problems and of national responsibilities – is one of the limits of politics, in Italy at any rate.

Today the violence of war lies within the reach of many peoples, groups, and obscure networks. Many of them can make war, but just as many have the possibility of preventing conflict. You have to work to repair the social fabric torn by political and economic conflict. There's a need for renewed reflection on the movements of reconciliation and nonviolence in this new context. Actually I'm a little mistrustful of overly rigid generalizations in this area, because often we can only feel our way in a world that is familiar with deep and tragic changes: the Gulf war, the war in the former Yugoslavia, the civil wars of Rwanda and Burundi, the current crisis in Zaire... are aspects of enormous changes going on that we can master, even with the help of reason, only in part.

And this is the framework in which to put the work for Mozambique?

Chronologically, our first effort in this area took place in Lebanon, at the beginning of the '80s, when we obtained the return of Christian groups in the Chouf and the liberation of some besieged villages after a meeting with

Walid Jumblatt at Sant'Egidio. Then there are some less well-known initiatives.

I'm convinced that a body like our community can do its part to set up contacts for peace. Obviously we're not the UN, and we don't have the ambition to get involved everywhere, or to act as mediators or facilitators in all the conflicts that surround us. The choice of Mozambique was forced on us because we had connections with this country. As I said, we were cooperating there; there were many ties of friendship, and we realized that development was impossible without peace.

The initiative came from Sant'Egidio, which then managed to attract the interest of the Italian government. How did you go about it?

Italy played an important role in Mozambique. It was the country's leading partner at the level of international cooperation, and it had significant economic leverage at its disposal. Plus, the Italian Communist Party was greatly interested in Mozambique. We initially took part in cooperative projects. But we wanted the collaboration focussed, efficient, directly in touch with the civilian population, not cathedrals in the desert. But in the end all this, all the cooperation, was insufficient if not useless. When the collaboration was ultimately shown to be going nowhere, we took this into account and got in touch with the people in charge of the guerrillas. We had strong, clear connections with the ruling class and the political class of Mozambique. But we had to get the other side, the guerrillas, involved. We kept la Farnesina, the Ministry of Foreign Affairs, constantly up to date about these contacts. Among other things they were indispensable in getting permission for the guerrllas, who had no passports, to enter Italy. The idea of informal meetings at Sant'Egidio came from the guerrillas. Gradually a special team of mediators was put together, coordinated by a former Italian undersecretary of State, a parliamentarian well known in Mozambique, who was appointed by the Italian government. Also taking part in it were two members of the community, Father Matteo Zuppi[1] and myself, along with the Archbishop of Beira. Everyone had his part to play: the representative of the Italian government reassured the government of Mozambique; the Archbishop reassured the guerrillas; as for us, in some way we functioned as a bridge. This created a synergy that a year later was joined by observers from France, Great Britain, the USA, Portugal, and the United Nations, who gave their guarantee to the negotiations. The USA and Portugal really cooperated to the limit, not at the negotiating table, but alongside it. The others stayed on the observer level. Then, finally, the whole affair, whose initiative had been Mozambican and Italian, passed to the UN.

In 1993, Boutros Boutros-Ghali defined Sant'-Egidio's method for peace in this way:

"The Community of Sant'Egidio has developed techniques that differ from, but at the same time are complementary to, those employed by professional peacemakers. In Mozambique the Community has worked discreetly for years with the goal of having the two parties meet. It made good use of its contacts. It was especially effective in getting others involved so as to contribute to a solution. It put into play its techniques, which are characterized by discretion and informality, together and in harmony with the official work carried on by the governments and intergovernmental organizations. On the basis of the experience in Mozambique the expression 'the Italian formula' was coined to describe this mixture, unique of its kind, of efforts for peace, by government and people outside government. The respect for the parties in the conflict, for those who are involved on the spot, is basic to the success of such initiatives."

When the accords were signed, on October 4, 1992, the feast of St Francis of Assisi, we decided to withdraw. We had played our role and done our part; things could move on in the hands of the UN. Naturally, when the crisis reopened, on the occasion of the elections of 1994, Father Matteo Zuppi returned to Mozambique, because we were known and esteemed there. We enjoyed real authority that, even at that time, when the electoral process threatened to explode, proved to be decisive.

Why limit your activity to Mozambique? This effort was due in large part to accident, it was linked to your history. But wouldn't it be better to get out of this mode of proceeding and develop instead a more "scientific" commitment, to choose your field of action early on, for example Peru, which, even more than Mozambique, has a double culture, Catholic and Marxist, or Chiapas in Mexico or, once again, Rwanda?

Mozambique revealed to the community energies whose power, whose very existence, it was unaware of.[2] The civilian population almost always wants peace, vehemently. The problem is that the political road to peace often can't be found. Our role, relatively speaking, was to channel the will of the people. But we were already present in Mozambique; and the government was already familiar with us, because we had assisted the rapprochement between Church and State, thanks to the interest of the Italian Communist Party: its secretary general, Enrico Berlinguer, came twice to Sant'Egidio, at our request, to meet Monsignor Gonçalves, the Archbishop of Beira. There was, in a word, a period of preparation, I don't think you can just drop out of the sky, like parachutists, into conflicts, as specialists or wizards of peace. Still we're closely following the situation in Angola on this score: we have contacts with the government and with UNITA, and we've welcomed here at Sant'Egidio two delegations, one from UNITA, the other from the government. Our house is beginning to become the landing place for a sort of pilgrimage from Africa: among those who have come here are the presidents of Burundi and Mozambique, the ministers of foreign affairs from Eritrea and Mozambique, the prime minister of Zaire, and others. At this moment, Burundi is very much on our minds. Recently – last summer, in fact – the ex-president of Tanzania, Julius Nyerere and the American diplomat assigned to the problems of the Great African Lakes region, Howard Wolpe, have made long stays together at Sant'Egidio, to mount a strategy capable of reawakening political dialogue in Burundi and averting a brutal war. The effort, with further commitment, is still under way, even if the picture of the crisis remains worrisome. The situation in the region of the Great Lakes is an unheard-of tragedy. There's a danger that we may be witnessing the dissolution of governments and mass exoduses with the butchery of hundreds of thousands of people. The disintegration of Zaire represents the crisis of an "empire", with disastrous consequences.

For years now Guatemala too has been the object of the Community's efforts for peace. The negotiations between the government and the URNG (the guerrillas), even though they started at the beginning of the '90s, were going slowly and threatened to stall. Among the main causes of this was the lack of direct and trustful conversation between the president's office and the commandants of the URNG. In the spring of 1995 the Community encouraged a face-to-face meeting at Sant'Egidio and in Paris between then-president Ramiro De León Carpio and the guerrilla commandants. We saw that direct communication speeded up the negotiations and made it possible to overcome many difficulties.

This story isn't very well known. How has it been coming along?

A few months after the events I mentioned there was voting for the presidential elections in Guatemala. We got into touch with Álvaro Arzú, the candidate who was giving the best guarantees for peace; we suggested to him a meeting with the commandants. This took place on two occasions at our residence in San Salvador between the two rounds of voting. Then there were three more sessions after the election of Arzú to the presidency. At Sant'Egidio, in February 1996, in a joint communiqué the two sides announced the resumption of official negotiations, which were prodded ahead with the help of the UN and other organizations until the peace accord was signed on December 29, 1996. This put an end to a conflict that had lasted twenty-five years. But we don't want to play at being a "little UN". We have to keep the doors and windows open, to keep listening to all the pains of the world, close by and far away. That's the lesson I gather from this experience.

It's not up to us to choose our field of activity, but to welcome requests. That's how we got involved in the problems of the Sudan. In my opinion, this is one of the most difficult situations of our time, because we find ourselves facing an ethnic conflict, a conflict between North and South, that intersects a religious conflict between Muslims and Christians. There's been a lot of talk about Lebanon; and I think that that makes sense. But I believe that we need to talk a whole lot more about the Sudan. We're moving on the level of our contacts. Three years ago in several rounds of discussion we saw some of the protagonists, people from the South, along with Tourabi, the fundamentalist leader, who was received by the Holy Father as well.[3] He had come to Italy at the invitation of RAI, the Italian Broadcasting System. And then the head of the political and military opposition to the government of Khartoum, John Garang, was our guest for a number of days. We have to keep this door open, but without being obsessed with reproducing the model of Mozambique. We're not professional diplomats, although neither are we improvisers or "dilettantes", as the *Economist* claimed.

We weren't born mediators, but we want to take to heart the reasons and the sufferings of the victims, as did Paul VI, who defined himself as "the advocate of the poor". This is an essential objective, which mustn't be lost sight of. Thus, during the negotiations on Mozambique, some of us could stand up and even shout, "This is shameful! People are dying and you're having a discussion!" Still you have to understand that a process of reconciliation, unfortunately – and I mean unfortunately – calls for a considerable amount of time. During the negotiations on Mozambique, some missionaries were sceptical. They were living the tragedy in the first person, at close quarters. Sometimes they lost patience with us, and said: "But you're in Rome, eating and drinking". Here we'd negotiate for an hour, then spend two hours at a restaurant, and then go and have more discussions for another hour. This was true, in the strict sense. But our moral force during the negotiations was that we really were the voice, at times the only voice, of the population. I recall when, in agreement with the missionaries, we gathered many letters and petitions for peace, with thousands of names, from Mozambique. Glancing over it, the head of the RENAMO delegation found the signature of his father whom he hadn't seen for more than ten years.

No, we aren't trying to intervene everywhere, and we don't want to. Apart from everything else we couldn't do it; our resources are too limited. But our aspiration to peace is great. You have to accept the wound of not being able to work miracles. But at least you have prayer. There's no need to be obsessed with the idea of reproducing the same model of mediation everywhere. But I think that helping peace means carrying forward a small project with tenacity and, if possible, all the way to success.

Has your experience with Mozambique been studied by any diplomats, in Italy or anywhere else?

Yes, it's been examined and discussed. Roberto Morozzo Della Rocca has written a splendid book on the subject. We gave him all the documents, and he scrupulously reported everything. The subject has also been studied by an American diplomat, Cameron Hume.[4] I let myself take some pride in this: the accords signed were well made and well negotiated, thanks to the synergy that was created. In situations of this sort, you can't be content with sentimentalism, with a warm embrace and good-byes: reconciliation is a demanding process, even from a legal point of view. The experience of the United Nations, on the other hand, has been, on the whole, rather difficult. The fact that it's a large international bureaucracy weighs too heavily on it. You meet highly motivated persons there, and others whose work is ineffective. In any event it's a great institution; and it represents a least common denominator among governments, which is at times the only good thing left.[5]

Couldn't the method of Sant'Egidio be used in the former Yugoslavia, where we see an interweaving of religion, ethnicity, and nationalism?

Father Vincenzo Paglia has become passionately involved with the situation in the Balkans. Still, you have to be careful not to cause confusion. When there already are organizations in place to take care of certain problems, you shouldn't intervene in an untimely manner. That can cause confusion or a weakening in the efforts for peace, through possible diversions. We went through this problem with Mozambique: to start a crisis that wasted more than a month, all that Portugal had to do was to propose moving the negotiations to Lisbon. I've learned the necessity of prudence.

We simply set up contacts and defined a humanitarian

aid project, initially in the form of medical shipments destined for the Serbs, the Bosnian Muslims, the Croats, and the Albanians in the area, to show that our initiative was first and foremost humanitarian and transethnic. We were in touch with the Bosnians, the Serbs, and the Croats. We've been talking for years with the Serbian Church, not in a pro-Serbian posture, but for ecumenical motives, and because we've discovered that one of the specific problems with a negative impact in the Balkans has to do with the isolation of the Serbian religious world. But this is only one aspect of the problem, because there are all the others too: Kosovo, Macedonia, Albania.

Some representatives from Kosovo have come to visit us a number of times, because this region is a true powder keg. I believe that reconciliation in Kosovo is a necessary process. It has to be achieved by reconciling what today seems irreconcilable, building some kind of coexistence between the Albanian majority and the Serbian minority. As we know, on September 1, 1996 a first accord was signed by Serbian president Milosevic and the Albanian leader of Kosovo, Rugova. This was worked out in roughly one year of work by the Community, and it reopens the educational system to the Albanian population after it had been totally closed for five years.

Implementing the accord remains difficult. On the other hand, it's no surprise if you recall that immediately after this – for different reasons – the most impressive protest yet broke out in the homeland of the Milosevic regime; and in 1997 the Albanian crisis exploded. There's also the case of Macedonia, a country that in my opinion should be more strongly supported. I've visited Macedonia; and I recall the line by President Gligorov (who later was the target of a serious assassination attempt): "It's not easy to stay human in the Balkans". I think, for example, that an agreement could be reached between Italy, Turkey, and various Balkan countries to rebuild the famous Via Egnatia, which linked Albania (or rather

Apulia) to Byzantium. It's not just a matter of public works. I think that some such bond ought to be reconstructed because of the risk these countries run of falling into the machinery of war, at times not even by their own choice. Sarajevo could become the epicentre of an earthquake that would run from Kosovo to Macedonia, all the way to Albania, an important country that, as we know, has had a particularly tragic experience.

The problem is to rebuild the harbours, in every sense.

I was in Albania during the last days of the Communist regime, shortly after the death of the dictator Enver Hoxha in 1985. Some university friends and I set up an experimental dialogue with Albanian culture in Bari, in the name of the assassinated hero, Gurakugi, with the goal of making contact with a few intellectuals.[6] This initiative had nothing to do with the Church. Then we took a trip, in the course of which I tried to meet the only Albanian bishop who had survived. Back then Albania was truly the Mount Athos of atheism, with its incredible human devastation. I still have some sad memories of it: no other communist country has endured the same experience. Then history resumed its course, in 1990-1991. But the old tensions resurfaced; and mistakes were made, while there still was a possibility of inaugurating brotherly relations between Catholics and Orthodox. In those days we thought about what would have been a very important package of Christian charity with help for both confessions, but in the end it couldn't be done. Today Albania occupies a strategic position because of its influence on Kosovo and on the Albanians of Macedonia. It's indispensable to build a chain of stability south of Bosnia. The community of Sant'Egidio does much work in Albania: social welfare, sanitation, education... It's a country that has to be rebuilt after the profound devastation caused by almost half a century of "real communism". I found the books by Elisabeth and Jean-Paul Champeix valuable for understanding the logic of desperation in which this country has lived. The myth of the besieged citadel, with its revolutionary purity, was common coin. The "new world" had to be born by force in Albania. These are topics and problems to be analyzed and rethought. I've known Albanians who despite everything still believed in the regime. After its fall I could observe great crises of conscience and a terrible void, of the sort that comes after a loss of faith. The death of the mystique of communism bore within itself a kind of secularization – a postcommunist secularization...[7]

What do you think about the current explosion of violence in Albania?

Political pluralism and the market economy are not magic words. They call for a slow transformation, which has been missing in Albania. The people have had the sensation of being swindled: the elections, the crisis unleashed by the pyramid schemes, the authoritarian systems of government, the corruption... And so Albanians have taken up their guns again, ransacking the arms depots. At this point the only arguments that remain convincing are about defending yourself, your family, and your clan. The state and a national consensus will have to be built around this. The bipolar tension between socialists and democrats has accentuated the splits and the clashes, the whole North-South division. You have to create the sense of a shared national destiny. This won't be easy now that the people have lost confidence in both the communist and the postcommunist governments.

Is peace in the Balkans possible, or is it a sort of act of faith and utopian hope?

I think it's a duty. But this prompts me to say something about the foreign policy of Italy. In the past people used to say that Italy was the "Bulgaria of NATO". That wasn't true. In fact, Italy managed to choose some major alignments toward the West, while having a strong internal communist party, and Europe... But today, when Italy could use an active foreign policy, we find ourselves handicapped by major problems. I wonder if we shouldn't introduce the concept of areas of responsibility, not in the hegemonic but the humanitarian sense. An area of responsibility could be shared with other countries. One such area, for example, is the Balkans, especially the southern Balkans, for Italy.

Does this mean a duty to interfere?

There's a lot of talk about interference, but often it's just a rite of impotence. It's undoubtedly better to take seriously the realization that one has no power. Political means must always prevail over armaments, over the military path. Military interference, even with a humanitarian goal, often leads to its own failure. I share the idea expressed by Mahatma Gandhi: "If there is to be a winner, victory will only be a living death for the nation that emerges victorious from the war". It seems to me that this applies to the problem. I'm not a military strategist, but I often reflect on the consequences of the Gulf War. Today we face a weakened Iraq, but a strengthened Saddam Hussein, a Kurdistan no longer under Iraqi control, but with an all-out struggle among the Kurds, where the Christian minority barely gets by in ever more difficult conditions. (We never talk about the Christian minorities, but here it seems to me simple honesty to mention one, out of respect for the truth.) The struggle among the Kurds, between Barzani and Talabani,[8] who have won some autonomous space, represents a tragic moment in the history of a people that never succeeded in having a political identity or freedom. I believe that it would be better to put coherent policies into place than to send soldiers. Otherwise you end up the way they did in Somalia. The case of Somalia is no doubt one of the unhappiest. It's had a terrible "anti-educational effect", because it's led people in America and the world – after the illusion of the first triumphal images of Operation Restore Hope – to believe that nothing can be done in Africa. The consequences have spilled far beyond the borders of Somalia. All of Africa has seen the powerlessness of military intervention, which has strengthened the enemies of peace, and not just in the Horn of Africa. It was a very clear demonstration of powerlessness. In reality the Italian experience suggested that you mustn't launch out on this sort of operation. The Italians have heavy responsibilities in Somalia, but they know the territory. Matteo Zuppi has met many delegations of Somalis, from different sides, each one of which always exalts its own particular solution. But the situation doesn't change. I distrust foreign policies launched to satisfy and reinforce the emotions of one's own public opinion. It's preferable not to base policy on emotion; peace is hard to build entirely on feelings. Here, it seems to me, is the source of the ambiguity of some humanitarian interventions: there's little policy and a lot of theatre.

Before undertaking any humanitarian intervention of any sort, you have to define a solid policy for peace. Soldiers don't miraculously bring peace. No intervention can be excluded on principle, but you need to reflect carefully on the conditions in which it will be carried out. Ideally it must help people to retake control of their own destiny, help the state to be reborn, and help the nation to escape the threat of war. Interference by humanitarian, not governmental, organizations grows out of a different kind of language, since this doesn't serve as a cloak for military intervention. The intervention of the NGOs, the non-governmental organizations, in the world, for strictly humanitarian purposes, takes its origin from a movement of conscience. I have known many people disposed to make sacrifices, courageous people who risked their lives for others. This is an aspect of Europe that it's good not to forget. It's a lovely expression of our civilization, which is one of effusion, that is, it doesn't live all hunched over itself, but for the sake of others. This may go back to Christian roots: living not for oneself but for him who has died and risen. These roots are – perhaps – also secular, as is shown by groups such as the *Médecins sans Frontières*; but surely here is the expression of a peculiar and authentically European conscience. Europe is a great laboratory of humanitarian policies.

With whom can you enter into dialogue? Can you, should you negotiate with everyone, beyond any moral considerations?

Every dialogue involves the risk of becoming someone's tool, this is true. But I remain deeply affected by Paul VI's encyclical *Ecclesiam suam* (1964), an extraordinary text, because it's full of confidence in human beings and in the Word. For me it's the *Magna Carta* of dialogue, dialogue of the Church and of Christians *par excellence*. Paul VI said: "The atmosphere of dialogue is friendship and, above all, service."

Unfortunately, sometimes one does find oneself facing men who have lost all sense of humanity, facing barbarians: the history of the 20th century is rich in acts of barbarism, to this day. In such cases must you, can you enter into dialogue?

What did St Francis do in the face of the lords of war? There's the episode of the wolf of Gubbio, in which he recognized – and the modern historiographer sees it the same way – not an animal, but a warmonger who terrorized the poor people of Gubbio. Francis talks to it and tames it. No one can be defined as a barbarian or evil to the point that he doesn't deserve even a word. You have to think of Jesus' relations with the people possessed by demons or with those who wanted to use him. At bottom, if you love only those who love you, if you discuss only with those who think the way you do, what merit is there in that? I don't think this is theoretical language: there's a Christian anthropological demand that we can't forget. And Francis, when he pushed beyond the Crusaders' camp to go and talk with the Sultan Malek-el-Kamel – the famous meeting in Damietta – was doing something that his contemporaries saw as madness, on the edge of treason. If it was madness, it was a holy madness.

What can be said about dialogue? At the time of the negotiations on Mozambique, I had people telling me: "You dialogue with guerrillas, but they're just bandits". To be sure, they were persons responsible for acts of violence, and I knew it. "They're using you", I was told. Well, I think that Christians have to be simple as doves, but also as wise as serpents. This requires culture, sensitivity, caution. Prudence too is made of culture and not of prejudices. But we can't accept interdicts, because the absence of dialogue creates the conditions for isolation, radicalization, and hatred, as the cases of Serbia and Iraq show. Certainly dialogue can also be "muscular" and hard. Here's where the problem of language comes in. We Christians are people of the word; we don't have any other weapons, but it *is* a force. I would define myself as a partisan of dialogue to the bitter end. Still it's not easy, because dialogue demands a reaching out to the other. You have to try to understand him, to help him get out of his own system. Paul VI said that we Christians are "experts in humanity". We acquire this sort of experience because every Church is a treasure of life. For example, it's enough to think of the extraordinary experience of the missionaries, of the twinning between some Churches of the North and the South. On the other hand, TV comes along to weaken the sense of dialogue, giving us information without dialogue, while we think we know because we see. But the issue here is another kind of speech.

Can you see without knowing?

Yes, seeing without knowing. On the contrary, dialogue leads us to see *and* to know. And then every person always succeeds in convincing me a little. Maybe I'm naive, but every time I talk with someone I have the sensation of recognizing a fragment of truth, even in the worst cases.

Aren't there extreme cases in which dialogue isn't possible, not even for the Christian? Can you dialogue with the commandants and torturers of the Nazi concentration camps? Can you dialogue with a Hans Frank, the gauleiter of occupied Poland, with the man in charge of Auschwitz?

I've never had to confront a situation like that. I might answer that if someone had talked with Frank before, perhaps he wouldn't have become exactly what he did become. But I wouldn't risk a hypothesis like that. Some brave bishops did talk with the Nazis to save human lives... In any event I don't want to make such an extreme case. I would only like to say: let's be careful not to draw up categories of persons with whom dialogue is out of the question. Didn't we have this problem with the communists? For decades didn't people say – and act accordingly – that there was no need to talk with them? For years many believed that dialogue was impossible, because the communists, intelligent as they are, used everything for their own ends. This was true, but it's also true that all politics to some extent uses the method of exploitation, at least to maintain consensus. I myself, by contrast, was deeply impressed by the method perfectly described in the simple but fundamental words of John XXIII: "Search for what unifies and put aside whatever divides". It's true that sometimes I don't want to meet this or that person. But you have to struggle against the prejudices rooted in us, even and especially against the strongest of these.

The spirit of St Francis seems to help you. Is there a spirit of Assisi?

Yes, there is a spirit of Assisi. It inherits the pioneering attempts at dialogue between the religions that have taken place from the congress in Chicago over a century ago onwards, until this process became a part of the Second Vatican Council. But what does the Assisi conversation consist of? It's a matter of reuniting all the religions, of presenting the Catholic Church as a servant of dialogue and of highlighting the weak strength of the religions, which is born not from power, from economic or political means, but from prayer and spiritual persuasion. That's the spirit of Assisi. That's why we thought in 1987 – though some were opposed to the idea – that we should continue the experiment started by Pope John Paul II the year before, peculiar to Assisi. This, in our opinion, couldn't be interrupted, because it had opened up a path of ecumenical dialogue and had created the conditions for a commitment to peace. I especially insist on ecumenical dialogue: when I saw Christians side by side with Muslims and Buddhists, I told myself and commented to others, referring to the Churches: "How little divides them, how much unites them!"

Today a sort of family has been born, a group of *aficionados*. That's how I discovered that for this or that religious leader leaving his country, meeting other people in charge of other religions, becoming interested in different persons and religious situations means, at least in part, escaping the trap of nationalism and an "ethnic" vision of one's own religion. "I'm not the only one who's suffering", one learns. "My religion isn't the same thing as the world". It's a significant experience of universality. Assisi 1986 had to continue, especially since every religion conceals within itself the temptation to war, to violence, while the encounter with others brings out the good that lies at the bottom of each one of us.

Catholic fundamentalists, along with Monsignor Lefebvre, condemned the 1986 meeting in Assisi. They claimed that Catholicism, the only true religion, can't place itself on the same footing as the other religions, which are by definition false.

The meeting in Assisi was in fact a big problem for Bishop Lefebvre. And he wasn't the only one to oppose it. Others, no less extremist, rejected it. Despite that, Assisi transmits a new, serenely new, image, which has nothing of adventurism about it. To be sure, the Assisi proposal has to be understood in all its dimensions. The rejection by Monsignor Lefebvre isn't surprising, because Assisi is the continuation of Vatican II; it's the creative reception of *Nostra Aetate*. In my opinion, the icon of Assisi has a theological meaning that merits deciphering. There surely is a theology of Assisi, but it isn't, contrary to what the fundamentalists claim, syncretism. In Assisi people didn't pray together; they prayed alongside each other, each respecting the other. This was the point of the appeal John Paul II made to "liberate the spiritual energies". Thus Christianity is the leaven, a humble yeast, in a dough made up of the most diverse kinds of flour mixed together in mysterious process of history.

The path of "People and Religions" began after the World Day of Prayer that took place in Assisi in October, 1986.

At this meeting, called by John Paul II, participants came from the Christian Churches and non-Christian religions. But the itinerary of ecumenical dialogue has a long history. Over a century ago, in 1893 the World Parliament of Religions was inaugurated in Chicago, at the prompting of a Presbyterian minister and with the support of the North American Catholic Church. For some time afterwards the event had a certain resonance, but the idea of continuing the initiative came to grief on the mutual mistrust in religious and secular institutions. In the following decades, there weren't many opportunities for relations between the religions, though there was no lack of informal contacts. The decisive step on the part of Catholics was the declaration *Nostra Aetate* by the Second Vatican Council, which deals positively with relations between Christianity, Judaism, Islam and other world religions, offering a theological foundation and encouragement for ecumenical dialogue.

The prayer of Assisi in 1986 brought about a convergence in the paths of dialogue between the various world religions. Taking part in it were religious leaders from the different communities who, on different grounds, in one way or another represented their co-religionists. These people of religion were engaged in the prayer for peace and in the encounter. The next year the community of Sant'Egidio began to promote annual meetings (by means of the international Association "People and Religions"), which were celebrated in the spirit of Assisi and nurtured by efforts to develop concrete programmes and cultural deepening. These meetings have seen a growth in the number of participants and a refinement in the dialogue on major religious problems (such as prayer) as well as the issues of peace and coexistence (the former Yugoslavia, Africa, weapons...)

Here are the different stages of the path pursued after Assisi:

1. Rome, October 27, 1987: *Prayer at the Roots of Peace* (among the participants: Cardinals Glemp and Martini, the Jordanian Al-Sharif).
2. Rome, October 28, 1988: *People of Prayer in Search of Peace* (among the participants: Sheik el Nimr, the Grand Mufti of Jerusalem Saad al Din).
3. Warsaw-Birkenau, August 30-September 3, 1989: *No More War* (among the participants: the Rev Yamada, Sheik Sakouta, Monsignor Rossano, the Metropolitan Filarete of Minsk, the Armenian Patriarch Snork I).

4. Bari, September 25-28, 1990: *A Sea of Peace Between East and West* (among the participants: the Patriarch of Alexandria Parthenios, Rabbi Toaff).

5. Malta, October 8-10, 1991: *The Religions for a Sea of Peace* (among the participants: Boutros Boutros-Ghali, Chissano, the Armenian catholicos Karekine I, the Grand Mufti of Egypt Tantawi).

6. Louvain-Brussels, September 1-3, 1992: *Europe, the Religions and Peace* (among the participants: President Mugabe, Cardinal Martini, Patriarch Sabbah, the Armenian Patriarch Karekine).

7. Milan, September 22-25, 1993: *Human Lands and the Invocation of God* (among the participants: Mikhail Gorbachev, the Syrian Patriarch Zakka Iwas, the Grand Rabbi of Israel Meir Lau).

8. Assisi, September 10-13, 1994: *Testimonies of Peace* (among the participants: the president of Portugal Mario Soares, the Ethiopian Patriarch Paulos, the Israeli Yossi Belein, the Palestinian Feisal Husseini).

9. Jerusalem, August 27-29, 1995: *Together in Jerusalem* (participants: Jews, Christians, and Muslims in the Old City in Jerusalem).

10. Florence, October 22-25, 1995: *Earth and Heaven of Peace* (among the participants: the Armenian Patriarch of Cilicia Aram I, Lech Walesa, Corazón Aquino, Rabbi Cohen).

11. Rome, October 7-10, 1996: *Peace is the Name of God* (among the participants: Oscar Luigi Scalfaro, Jacques Santer, the world leaders of some of the main Jewish and Muslim organizations. The meeting was concluded, on the tenth anniversary of the first gathering in Assisi, by the secretary of state, Cardinal Angelo Sodano).

12. Padua and Venice, October 5-7, 1997: *Peace is the Name of God*. The final prayer for Peace was celebrated in Venice, highlighting the links between Eastern and Western countries. In Padua, at the opening session, the President of Rumania, Constantinescu, invited Sant'Egidio to organize the next World Meeting for Peace in Bucharest, which took place between August 30 and September 1, 1998.

Isn't the leaven Rome, rather than Christianity?

In a certain sense you could say that in Assisi in 1986 the Bishop of Rome was at the centre, as a sincere servant of this movement. But Rome isn't just Rome. There are two other directions. One is Assisi, in which St Francis lived as a frontier of witness of the Church of Rome. For this I hope – and here's a proposal that I've made for the Holy Year 2000 – that the pilgrims who come to Rome may, if they wish, pass through Assisi (this is possible, thanks to the expansion of the Perugia airport, which is close to Assisi). The other great direction is Subiaco and Monte Cassino, i.e., Benedictine monasticism. We can't forget that Cassino is a theatre of World War Two, something like a monument with a crown of cemeteries, containing the graves of more than 30,000 soldiers of various nationalities buried there. Franciscanism and Benedictine monasticism preached peace in a Europe that fought for centuries. These are two components that, in my view, are part of the soil of the witness borne by the Church of Rome. Rome is also located within an arc made up of Assisi, Subiaco, and Monte Cassino: between St Benedict and St Francis.

But let's return to talk about ecumenism. There's one supreme obligation, which is to seek unity. I'm convinced that the Church of Rome, if only for sociological reasons, has a chance to contribute a great deal to this search through dialogue between religions, in a spirit of mutual respect. I'm convinced that when people of religion meet and talk, a transformation occurs in them. It must also be said that these meetings have allowed the working out of a sort of ecumenical "liturgy": people listen to each other, they pray, close to one another but without blurring their identity, and they find themselves united in straining toward the same goal. These "liturgies" of unity are an important fact. You can also hear in them the voice of the victims, the voice of distress, the laments of the world's suffering, through these witnesses to pain who come from countries in great trouble and who speak to the people of religion. Here's another basic feature that has grown in these years after Assisi. It seems to me that here's something that helps to refine the sensitivity, the vulnerability, and the positive response of believers.

Religions have caused a lot of suffering at various points in history.

Religions *have* caused a lot of suffering, that's true; and they continue to cause suffering. It's a tragedy. Believers and – in a certain sense – religions have also suffered for their faith.

Wasn't there a risk of wearing the formula of Assisi out?

Yes and no. According to a very secularised logic, obsessed by quantifiable results, I would say "yes". Many wars continue on or break out: even though the movement for encounter and dialogue between the Religions has grown; in spite of the great prayer that ascends in many ways, and that, at least once a year, has the strength and intensity of the great religious traditions of the world, one beside the other.

I would say, however, that this is a rather superficial way of looking at all of

What has changed in these years?

In the '80s, it seemed impossible that a Jew and a Muslim could be together in the same place. Today, many have become friends and with great respect have seated themselves at the same table, in order to discover the reasons for a conflict, which is not written into the heart of the two religions.

Today, it is more difficult to make use of religions in the service of war. This is thanks to this continuing movement of encounters and initiatives, on a worldwide level, this movement of 'People and Religions'. In times in which religion can be petrol poured on conflicts between peoples and ethnic groups, this seems not a little to me. It seems also to me that, from these interreligious encounters, there might have been born a more profound knowledge of the vocations of the different religions, and this role has much to do with the 'weak strength' of faith and prayer as an additional resource for the world.

The interreligious dialogue, then, it seems to me, came from the enclosure of principal actors and specialists, and has become common, in many cases a grass roots fact, in many churches. The great ten-yearly convention of the Italian Church, which was held in Palermo, saw the presence of an evangelical, Jewish and Muslim delegation at the heart of the labours. Ten years ago it was unthinkable. This has created awareness in the entire Catholic Church that it can be placed at the service of others.

Is there any concrete example?

The last of the "People and Religions" convention, which was held in Bucharest in Rumania, has, in fact, illuminated the extraordinary potential of dialogue in the healing of the wounds of generations.

A year ago, at Padua, the Rumanian President Constantinescu, intervening at the meeting organised by the "Peace is the Name of God" community, threw out the suggestion that the World Prayer for Peace might be held this year in Rumania itself. This would mean the first time in a country that has a large Orthodox majority. An event of this importance without the agreement of the Orthodox Church would have been counterproductive, but at first sight one was dealing with an impossible task, given the tensions of recent years between the many Orthodox Churches and the Church of Rome. We had friendly relations with various representatives of the

Orthodox Churches who had also participated in other Prayer Meetings for Peace. It was thus possible to organise the convention in full collaboration with the Patriarcate of Rumania, which, for a number of faithful, is the second largest Church in the world of Orthodoxy. What happened was extraordinary, and it is not I who say it, but the Patriarch Theocist and other Orthodox Patriarchs.

Notwithstanding a severe strain in relations between the Greek Catholics and Orthodox in that country, for the first time the Patriarch was present and addressed the congregation taken the word in the Catholic Cathedral, for the first time Orthodox bishops have participated in the Greek-Catholic Liturgy, and never have oriental cardinals and patriarchs of the Church of Rome participated so solemnly and in such large numbers in moments of prayer and collaboration in an orthodox country – if one excepts the celebrations for the Millennium of Russia.

What has happened is a radical change of ethos in the relations between the two Churches, which from that of suspicion has passed through many stages to that of friendship and warmth. It seems to bring nearer the first journey of the pope in a country with an orthodox majority.

At the same time, it was also a panorthodox meeting (nearly all the Churches were present), brought about by an initiative undertaken by Catholics. I would say Catholics without any hidden agenda except dialogue and peace. And then, there have been other important facts, in the interreligious dialogue, but the most important of all has perhaps been this beginning of the thaw between Catholics and Orthodox in a time of great difficulty.

I would say: this is an ecumenism of the people and an authentic dialogue of life, of friendship, that seems to be able to fill some gaps which the dialogue of documents is apparently not able to heal. There is, in short, a new season to live – which is that of the ecumenism in life – in order to heal the distances and suspicions, both psychological and historical, even when those theological distances and suspicions seem incurable.

The notion of the "just war" remains present in Christian theology. Some bishops have recalled this on the occasion of the Gulf War; and John Paul II has mentioned it as one of the ways to save Bosnia.

I'm convinced that the Church's field of action is one of reason, peace, encounters. Men can always choose war, if they really want it; but it's for the Church to pray, to preach, to bear witness. I'm afraid, in fact, that some of the bishops may run the risk of identifying themselves with their country to the point of becoming wedded to its causes. I think of this especially à propos of the bishops of the former Yugoslavia. And there's hardly a shortage of examples even in the history of the western nations. You don't always have to say something about every conceivable topic. I think that sometimes the prophecy of silence is appropriate: *Jesus tacebat* ("Jesus was silent"). In the face of the vicissitudes of history, this forgotten dimension must have its importance restored. At times silence can be something other than shame or a dodge.

The Church can't say everything and know everything. There's a time to speak out and a time to be silent. Besides, silence can be a time of prayer: you entrust to the Lord your own powerlessness and confusion. It's also a prophetic gesture. At times, to be sure – "for the love of Zion" – as we read in the book of the prophet Isaiah – we can't keep silent. I remember how John XXIII, in a period of conflict, was inspired by the silence of Jacob, "who among his sons was content to look, to suffer, and to be silent. *Pater vero rem tacitus considerabat*". Sometimes we're only too ready to speak believing that our words leave a mark. I often have the impression that in the Churches too many documents get published: there are good ones, complete ones, but not all of them may be necessary. There's no need to banalize and humiliate the word, which remains something fundamental. But the word – and the Word of God – speaks in silence. There's also a time to be silent.

NOTES

1 Matteo Zuppi, a Roman priest born in 1955, comes from a family that has worked for the Holy See. His father was editor of *L'Osservatore Romano*. At Sant'Egidio he is concerned with the developing countries, especially in Africa.

2 A solid study of Sant'Egidio's international action may be found in R. Morozzo Della Rocca, "Sant'Egidio: la via romana alla pace", in *Limes* 3 (1993), pp. 69-82.

3 In southern Sudan various groups are struggling against the government in Khartoum. Among these groups are the SPLM/A (Sudanese People's Liberation Movement/Army) and the SPLM/A United (which is divided into numerous factions). Tourabi, the fundamentalist leader of the Islamic North, though he doesn't have any official role, seems to be the strong man in the northern balance of power.

4 C. Hume, *Ending Mozambique's War* (Washington, 1994); R. Morozzo Della Rocca, *Mozambico. Dalla guerra alla pace* (Cinisello Balsamo, 1994).

5 See *Les Nations Unies et le Mozambique: 1992-1995*, with an introduction by Boutros Boutros-Ghali (New York, 1995).

6 The colloquy gave rise to a publication, *L'omicidio politico di Luigi Gurakugi. Vrasja Politike e Luigi Gurakugi* (Bari, 1988). Andrea Riccardi read a paper there, "L'Oriente sotto casa. L'Albania vista dall'Italia tra gli anni '20 e '30", pp. 45-72.

7 E. and J.P. Champeix, *57 Boulevard Staline. Chroniques albanaises* (Paris, 1990) and *L'Albanie ou la logique du désespoir* (Paris, 1992).

8 The most substantial political groups in Iraqi Kurdistan are the Kurdish Democratic Party, whose president is Massoud Barzani, and the Patriotic Union of Kurdistan, whose president is Jalal Talabani.

CHAPTER FOUR

Between the Mediterranean and Europe

The question of the Mediterranean is very much alive at Sant'Egidio. What does the Mediterranean mean to you?

The Mediterranean is our world. We've talked at length about Sant'Egidio as a Roman reality. Now I'm talking about Italy: we find ourselves between two great political – but also religious – realities, Europe and the Mediterranean. It's not quite right to say that the Mediterranean is purely European. That's imprecise, because we aren't Germans, but Italians; that is, we're Mediterranean Europeans. These two realities, Europe and the Mediterranean, are things that we experience deeply together. Now to say that Italy must concern itself only with Europe means to forget our original way of being European. But also, to say that Italy must concern itself only with the Mediterranean would be eccentric. In the past the seas didn't divide, they unified; it was the mountains that separated. This is clear to anyone who reads Fernand Braudel's *The Mediterranean and the Mediterranean World in the time of Philip II*[1]. The distance between Paris and Genoa may be greater than between Genoa and Algiers. But in our day all this has been forgotten. You have to re-read the history of the relations between the Mediterranean countries. The tragedy of the Mediterranean is that we experience it as the lake of the Cold War, and we've lost the sense of its unity. But if you go to Apulia, it looks as if Albania and Greece aren't far away. The same thing happens in Morocco and Spain. In any event, the problems are anything but simple.

Nowadays the problem of a "new Yalta" has arisen, that is, a division between the Islamic South and the European North, with Israel thought of as a western outpost. The Mediterranean countries of Europe don't have a clear vision of the southern, Muslim shore. They foresee a separation on many levels, and reasons of security aren't the final ones. This schema is a mistake, because we Mediterraneans have in common a material culture, a lifestyle, a way of being. Writers should say something about the unity and diversity of Mediterranean civilization.

The Mediterranean has a unitary civilization, but it's also the contact-zone between the North and the South, the place where Islam can become the ideology of the South's revolt against the North. If so, a new boundary, a new frontier, would be created, with a few buffer states like Turkey, Israel, and Morocco. While rumours of war echo and re-echo through the nations of the Mediterranean, I'd like to insist on our common destiny. The religions form part of this destiny; and ecumenical dialogue is one of the keys to it, even if we have to acknowledge that not too many people really believe in dialogue between Christianity and Islam. True, it's an extremely complex dialogue, and the problems can't be resolved by a couple of meetings. But it's one thing to accept the complexity of the dialogue, and another to cross it off as useless or impossible.

Our idea of the Mediterranean can largely be summed up in the conviction that an intra-Mediterranean dialogue is possible. There are affinities between a Sicilian, an Egyptian, and an Algerian. It's enough to go to Sicily to realize this. That's how we understood that Algeria wasn't far away. We've already seen how our initiatives are never taken just so, by chance, but are integrated into a fabric, into a history that induces us to make certain choices. Algeria and Italy, then, are in the heart of the Mediterranean, neighbours across the way, so to speak. And Italy – no secondary factor here – depends greatly on Algeria for its energy resources.

The Mediterranean also means Greek Orthodoxy, which is characterized by a certain intolerance, juxtaposed as it is with Muslim Turkey, which is pointed toward Europe but at the same time led by an Islamic government.

There are different attitudes in Orthodoxy: one looks westward, the other eastward. In Russia there's St Petersburg, and there's Moscow. And Greek Orthodoxy has both these souls: one, more withdrawn into itself, is the Athens-Belgrade axis; the other, open to ecumenism and looking toward the Mediterranean, is the Fanar, the ecumenical patriarchate; it's Constantinople. Perhaps it would be more correct to say that these two souls exist in every Church.

At Sant'Egidio we feel strongly the force of attraction of Orthodoxy and the East; we experience a kind of veneration for this Orthodox Eastern world, which enters into our prayers and into the presence of the icons.

And through Santa Maria in Trastevere.

Yes. Santa Maria in Trastevere has deep traces of Byzantium and bears the imprint of the undivided Church. We keep there the icon of Clemency and Peace, which was painted between the 7th and 8th centuries in the Byzantine style, but with an inscription in Latin, the expression of diverse cultural confluences. The mosaic in the apse, part of which goes back to the 12th and part to the 13th century, picks up the Byzantine artistic tradition again, even though with some more western elements of perspective.

We took our first ecumenical trip to Istanbul five weeks after the death of Patriarch Athenagoras. Patriarch Dimitrios then came to Sant'Egidio, and later – in the last few years – Patriarch Bartholomeos paid us a visit here and in Belgium. We maintain a strong bond with Orthodoxy, especially through its liturgy. In the West we have, perhaps, made our liturgy too intellectual:

"Everything is rational" or is supposed to be. People have forgotten or stopped stressing that liturgy is a celebration of glory, and that's not just the splendour, but also the profundity, of the divine mystery. This problem doesn't come from the recent liturgical reform. It's a mode of rationalization that was already present in the mass of Pius V. The problem is an ancient one: it seems to me to come from the break with the Byzantine East and from centuries of a lack of exchanges, a fact that has undoubtedly led to mutual impoverishment. Something like this, in fact, may have taken place in the Byzantine and pre-Chalcedonian East as well.

To advance along the road of ecumenism it would help enormously to develop a sense of brotherliness among the five great patriarchs: of Rome, Constantinople, Antioch, Jerusalem, and Alexandria. They made up the five cardinal points of the undivided Church of the first millennium, and I think we have to start out from there. Nevertheless, if there's a great Orthodox *ecumene*, we mustn't ignore the fact that there's also a nationalistic current: dialogue is important to prevent people from locking themselves up within their own frontiers. The great council of Constantinople of 1872 condemns "philethism", or the exclusive love of one's own nation.

"Philethism, that is, the distinction based on differences in ethnic origin and language, and the claim, or the exercise, of exclusive rights on the part of human individuals and groups of the same country and the same blood, can have some foundation in the secular States, but it's alien to our particular order... The majority of the Christian Churches founded in the beginning were local. They welcomed the faithful of a certain city or a certain region, without making distinctions of race... They were not designated by the ethnic origin of believers."[2]

The problem of relations between the Church and the nation remains a crucial fact for Orthodoxy in the 19th and 20th centuries. Because it's so crucial, Orthodoxy mustn't be left to itself. We have connections with the

Greeks, and we've chosen to maintain our ties with the Serbs as well. I'm struck by their passionate (I would call it "religious") love for the nation, something that, in those terms, isn't part of our tradition, neither in France nor in Italy nor, for that matter, in most western countries. I'm thinking, for example, of a Serbian bishop, a monk, a man of prayer and sacrifice, a great soul, but a great nationalist. Must he be isolated? Here's where we face the issue of the embargo, which has a spiritual and a human side, and which ultimately can't have satisfying results. Isolation, unfortunately, plays into the hands of the extremists. The history of the isolation of some Orthodox Churches has been a terrible one. I think of the Russian Churches after 1917. For this reason we can't underestimate the Russian ecumenical openings of the '60s, even if they came to maturation in a framework of very little freedom. Today the Russian Church is free and allows all its souls to express themselves. Communion and dialogue bring about the emergence in us of more humane elements, of what's best in us. I believe in dialogue, even with the hardest interlocutors. Besides, there are also intransigent Catholics. Speaking of the Orthodox Churches I realize that we have to have a more vital rapport with their world, a less episodic connection, and not just on the hierarchical level.

Do the European and Mediterranean conflicts also shed light on the division between the Churches?

The crises in eastern Europe and the war in the former Yugoslavia have forcefully stripped bare the terrible division, which is made up of incomprehension and an absence of communication. Without reconciliation among Christians there will never be a solid peace. We need the Orthodox world: I've always learned a lot from the Orthodox and from their prayers. I'm thinking of the role of the liturgy during the difficult years of the life of the Russian or Ukrainian people. Friendship and dialogue restore a vital communication and a circulation of gifts. I recall a conversation at Sant'Egidio with Oscar Cullmann on complementarity among the traditions of the Churches and on the need for reconciliation so that this richness can be fully expressed.[3] On the other hand, there's the weight of history. We don't have to despair just because so much work remains to be done, especially in some situations. Despair means closing oneself up, in a self-sufficient manner, in one's own denominational mode, and leaving ecumenism on the margins, as a well-mannered ecclesiastical diplomacy might. So, history itself, in its own way, challenges the Churches on unity.

We can't forget yet another Christian world that for centuries has remained outside both Orthodoxy and the Christian West. I'm thinking of the ancient Eastern Churches that didn't participate in or accept the Council of Chalcedon. Their history tells how stubbornly they took root in faith and in cultures that are neither Byzantine nor Latin: the Copts in Egypt, the Syrians, the Armenians, and the Ethiopians (the oldest African Church). Churches of the people and of monks... In Turkey I visited Tur Abdin, the "mountain of the servants of God", the pulsating heart of Syrian monasticism, now practically wiped out by political and military turmoil: there was still something left of that millenarian atmosphere. Furthermore, the Coptic Church – we're in touch with the monks and with the Patriarch Shenouda III – have experienced a great renaissance. These ancient Churches historically have known not power but humiliation (the case of Ethiopia is different). Nowadays emigration and a globalized world are certainly causing new problems. The Syrian Patriarch Zakka I Iwwas asked me: "Will we survive outside the Middle East?" And he concluded: "I hope that our people will remain Christians everywhere". Armenian history too is a tragic one. The Armenians are in a new stage of greater unity. The visit we made to Armenia (a part of the Soviet Union at the time) was after the earthquake of 1988, in order to show some concrete solidarity with them. At Sant'Egidio we welcomed the supreme Catholicos Kharekine, an old friend from the days when he was living in Lebanon. Their ecumenical commitment is very strong (the other Catholicos, Aram I, said the same thing). They're an important part of the history of Christianity, even if their numbers have been reduced. The non-Chalcedonian Churches provide different historical models of the "inculturation" of Christianity. The case of the Ethiopians is obvious, with their Semitic and African roots. Patriarch Paulos, who knows the United States well, along with various Ethiopian bishops, finds himself facing new choices in an Ethiopia no longer imperial or communist. How to remain faithful to a thousand-year-old tradition and live in modernity? It's a dilemma common to all the Churches, but quite particularly for these non-Chalcedonian communities, which have, in a certain sense, been closely tied to a single culture since time immemorial.

It's the problem of relations between faith and culture...

Much has been written and discussed on this question. Naturally in today's world what we call culture is something different from the culture against which the Christianity of the non-Chalcedonian Churches measures itself. I recall what Pietro Rossano wrote: "A faith that would accept being closed up in private and concealed in the secret places of the heart without becoming socialized, without acting on the external expressions of human beings and on the ways of promoting their individual and communal condition, would no longer be responding to the vital implications of the Christian message..." And he quoted the Letter of James: "Faith without works is dead" (2:17).

To return to the quadrant of Europe and the Mediterranean, could we say that, right now, to the south and north of this sea there are two ways of transcending nationhood?

There's a secular mode, that of the European Union, and a religious mode, which is that of Islam?

Experience teaches us that the nation is an essential object, useful and at times dangerous. In the Balkans and the former Yugoslavia, nationalities have been repressed, practically ignored; and today they are resurging in a violent fashion. Paraphrasing Lenin, I would say that nationalism is a childhood disease of the nation. There's an immense problem here. Talk about the Mediterranean is also talk about nations, which, however, must be overcome by the definition of a larger whole and not by being torn into sub-wholes coagulated around merely material or instinctive interests.

Going beyond the nation...

Yes, going beyond the nation. It's the experience of community: the person remains in the centre, but at the same time is engaged in something else that transcends him or her. I think that the European Union is in effect our secular way of going beyond the nation. In the face of the new Germany, the current and tepid Europeanism strikes me as a mistake. Until not very long ago there was a unity between Italy and Germany, because the Christian Democratic Union (the CDU) and the Italian Christian Democratic Party were sisters, just as Konrad Adenauer and Alcide De Gasperi were closely connected. We underestimated that Italian-German bond.

Today, on the contrary, we are backwards with respect to Europe. We seldom think in a European mode; or at least we think only of the European economy. Here's the weakness, because in doing so we leave France to form all by itself a difficult couple with Germany – even though this purely economic Europe is disappointing in so many ways. It doesn't have a face, as you can see not just in the Brussels bureaucracy, but also in the lack of political choices. In my opinion, the role of Italy remains fundamental. Initially I had a clearer perception of the Mediterranean than of Europe. But I have to say that, being a Mediterranean, thinking in a Mediterranean fashion, I discovered how essential Europe is. It's the reason why we mustn't leave Germany all by itself. I feel very anxious over the development of a certain Italian victimization-complex. All too often we think we're the victims, but in fact we're only victimizers. We saw this right after both the two World Wars. We regularly go through these phases of national self-pity. The Italian crisis has been dragging on for some years now.

Travelling through the world I realize that people have only a feeble grasp of the Italian situation. The image of our country abroad is a confused one. Italians are turning in on themselves. Besides, the system has been loudly cracking and splitting. *Newsweek* magazine recently published an alarming list of countries hit by the virus of corruption, including some European countries. Italy is right up there among the most corrupt, followed by Greece, South Korea, and Mexico. In Italy a strong reaction has sprung up against corruption, to the point that there's talk about a revolution against what Italians call *Tangentopoli* (Rake-off City). Still, within the country these days uncertainty prevails. Only yesterday there was, at bottom, the certainty of an international position: Italy was the democratic bulwark confronting the East. But now everything has rapidly changed, both inside and outside. That's true even though I think I can note – without having any nationalistic axe to grind – that today Italy must recover the sense of its responsibilities, including the international ones. There are specifically Italian problems, but these aren't unknown in the other countries of western Europe, which have no special immunity to them.

If we leave Germany by itself, with that immense world now opening up on its eastern flank, we are doing it and ourselves a great disservice. For the moment Germany can control itself, but the instinct of domination is ready – as ever – to take the upper hand. This isn't a question of blaming the Germans; the instinct of domination is also linked to the peculiar role of the nation and to the awareness that peoples have of it. That's why European identity is important. Nowadays it seems to me that some problems affecting France and Italy's friendship have been overcome. But it was a mistake to talk about a Rome-London axis pitted against a Paris-Bonn axis. Great Britain is a great country, an exemplary democracy, which gave us tremendous lessons during the war. But the ensemble of Italy, France, and Germany remains the pivot on which Europe is based, from the time of the "little Europe" of the Six, from the 1957 Treaty of Rome.

The other subject is Islam. Arab unity is a great myth capable of mobilizing the masses, but the unitary structures to underpin it don't exist. There are different national destinies. My Algerian friends have spoken to me of "Arab egoism", the national egoism of the Arabs. In this sense it seems to me that Islam, or the Arab world, hasn't succeeded yet in overcoming the idea of pure national interest in the face of international relations. This is what we've seen in the various wars against Israel: the force of national interest ranged against the Palestinian cause. Granted, at the time a certain pan-Arab rhetoric made it impossible to confront the problems with the necessary realism, including the realism imposed after the defeat. There are well-defined, structural national interests; and peace in the Middle East will be made on the basis of these interests: those of Israel, Egypt, the Palestinians, Jordan, and Syria.

Wouldn't it be the duty of Europe to come to the aid of the Mediterranean nations, voicing support for a Mediterranean ensemble that integrates the idea of the Arab nation and the European nation? On this point, it seems useful to me to mention Turkey, which is important, especially after the success of the fundamentalists at the polls. I would have liked a Turkey better integrated into the evolution of the region. Perhaps I still feel some nostalgia for cosmopolitan Istanbul, but this seems a value to me. I love cosmopolitanism. The way the empires have come to an end hasn't always been a gain for the world, because they once offered a way to reconcile the nations with a larger whole. True, we can't miss the fact that the ruling classes of the Austro-Hungarian empire were incapable of respecting national identities. By then those classes were near extinction. There are two histories at issue here, of course; but both developed within multinational frameworks in which many peoples had found themselves for centuries.

I'm not nostalgic for the Ottoman system; but from a historical standpoint you have to remember that in the face of an intolerant Europe, both Christians and Jews were able to live together in a Muslim confessional state. To be sure, they were second-class citizens, but they managed to live, something that in past centuries wasn't possible for Muslims in our midst. That's why I recall cosmopolitan Istanbul. I think of the old photographs of Istanbul, of Pera, with the Italians, the Levantines, the Greeks, the Armenians... Salonica, Sarajevo, and Jerusalem too were multinational Ottoman cities. Coexistence wasn't always easy, but people did live together. That's over now.

The same Austro-Hungarian framework had developed a system of coexistence, even if certain nationalities had no chance to express themselves. For obvious reasons, Italian culture during the Renaissance nurtured various grudges toward the Habsburg empire. Still, one can't help grasping the value of this civilization, though it was obviously doomed to go under in that political context. When you visit Trieste, a city without a hinterland, you sense something of that multinational atmosphere. Visiting Lvov, the old Austro-Hungarian Leopoli (then part of Poland, and after that of the USSR), I could appreciate the difficult but real coexistence that went on in the city before 1918: Ukrainians, Poles, Jews, Armenians.

But the Jews were exterminated by the Nazis during World War II, and a majority of the Poles moved west. I'm not idealizing the world of the past. I simply believe that we mustn't abandon ourselves to contemptuous judgements. History can restore our real sense of this coexistence between nations under an "imperial" power. That world was bound to disappear in the Europe of the nations, and it did.

With the end of the Soviet Union, the ultimate multinational empire has gone. The crises of the former Soviet nationalities belong to the legacy of the multinational empires: the national frontiers, with their ethnic rigidity, are irrelevant. This has been seen everywhere, from Anatolia to Bosnia and Moldavia. The multiracial nature of the empires was based on a national, political, and cultural hegemony. To be sure, the Habsburgs were more refined... Nowadays the processes of multinational integration pass through quite different institutional and political frameworks. "Nations don't die", said Pope Benedict XV (1914-1922), who had lived through the surge of nationalism at the end of the empires. And he was right. We've seen this in eastern Europe after the end of communist regimes. But it's also true, and not in a contradictory but a complementary way, that the nations need forms of association: history, the economy, the movements of population, emigration all thrust in this direction.

And present-day Turkey?

I think that Atatürk built something important, but I wonder if he didn't make a mistake by totally destroying cosmopolitanism. Perhaps it was inevitable, otherwise Turkey could never have been born. But Anatolia remains a complicated question. We still see this today, with the Kurds, the Islamic brotherhoods, Islamic fundamentalists, and nationalists. This country isn't just Turkish, it isn't just national. The current electoral success of the fundamentalists in Turkey is the sign of a disturbing grassroots revolt against a process of homogenization. Despite this, I'm convinced that Turkey will hold up well. And we badly need Turkey. Not as a country to serve as a policeman against the communists (who no longer exist), not as a secular Turkey taking sides against fundamentalism – one more misinterpretation – nor as a Turkey whose job is to dominate formerly Soviet Muslim Asia (besides, I'm not so sure that it has the economic wherewithal to do that). I think we need a Turkey that represents a piece of our Europe. I'm afraid you'll never have complete peace in the Balkans without its participation. In fact, eastern Europe has two poles, two souls: the Ottoman pole, so to speak (less important, to be sure) and the Slavic pole. Here too is why, for so many historical reasons, Turkey is a part of our Europe. That's why the Turkish-Greek nationalistic clash is insane. Europe mustn't have to chose, and mustn't put itself into a situation where it has to choose between Greece and Turkey. A divided Cyprus, where tensions run high, is the acid test of this. We have to work to reconcile Greeks and Turks. On the other hand, I don't share the position taken by the European prime ministers, tied to the popular principle that Turkey can never enter Europe because it's Muslim. What reason is there to raise a barrier and not negotiate the conditions? This amounts to abandoning Turkey and weakening its western roots. Turkey can't go far away, because it's our neighbour. But what kind of neighbour will we have?

Could you make analogous observations about Morocco?

Perhaps you could, and for Tunisia as well. Still, Morocco has had a different historical and cultural role, far different from Turkey's. With Turkey, to some extent, we share the Balkans. Morocco is outside Europe, even on the cultural plane, despite the many ties that have been woven between us. Turkey is a frontier zone, like Greece. And we mustn't forget Greece itself, which is very important. We Europeans sometimes confuse the Greece of history, the Greece of today, and the Greece of classical culture. To this last Greece we arbitrarily attribute the geographical collocation of present-day Greece, while we know that Greek culture developed between Anatolia and Greece.

Are you speaking in favour of the multi-ethnic State?

I believe that to achieve a peaceful equilibrium you need subjects. The nations are the best subjects we have found, in history, to allow the identities of people to express themselves and to establish a balance among them. I'm not a federalist, but I harbour great respect for the inter-ethnic state, such as, for example, the Ottoman empire or the USA or the Austro-Hungarian empire. We have to admit that nowadays all of these have vanished except for America. Many inter-ethnic models are irreconcilable with national self-assertion. You could also look to South Africa, which today has taken up a challenge of great importance for all of Africa. Moreover, many states in Africa are going through serious problems of coexistence among different ethnic groups. Because of immigration the question of inter-ethnic coexistence is being raised in the majority of European countries, including France, Germany, Italy, and England.

We have to be careful not to confuse nationality and ethnicity, so as not to wind up multiplying micro-states. The road to respect for pluralism doesn't pass through the creation of new but fragile states. Part of the tragedy of decolonialization was the way it created weak states, whose future and whose frontiers were insecure. A nation – as John Paul II said to the UN – can also live without the state, provided that its fundamental characteristics are respected.

Might the evolution of Belgium, where the community of Sant'Egidio has a presence, allow us to probe a bit into this dilemma?

What's happening in Belgium, with the exacerbation of national interests, is very dangerous. I've seen it up close, in contact with our friends from the community in Antwerp. They pray at the same time in Flemish and in French. If someone is a Francophone, he or she prays in French; if he or she is a Fleming, in Flemish. But it's the same prayer, not two prayers in two different places. The Flemings speak Flemish, the Francophones respond in French. I realized that the experience of Sant'Egidio has also allowed them to rediscover their sense of Belgium. Through an in-depth reflection they've come to understand the opportunity that Belgium represents: as Belgians, if they are Flemings, hence rooted in the world loaded with sensitivity and tradition that is the Flemish connection with Holland; but also if they are Walloons, and hence engaged in the French-speaking world, which offers a broader perspective.

Belgium too has a role to play in the world. In order to count in the world, to exist, to be more than just merchants, we have to be Belgians – said King Baudouin. This spirit of openness of the members of our community is all the more interesting when you consider that many of them, before they joined, were extremely pro-Flemish and refused to accept multilingualism. That is, until the moment when they raised the concrete issue of what language was to be used in the community. Today I realize that Belgium can't simply be defined by the relations between the two majority nations: there are also the Germans and the Italian immigrants. And we can't forget the North Africans. It's a multi-ethnic state, not just a binary one.

At this moment Belgium is going through an extraordinary period, as its citizens react deeply and straightforwardly to the scandal of their public life. The "scandals" are a phenomenon of this season. But the Belgian response has had its own originality, starting out with the defence of children and of life itself. It will be interesting to see how this evolves, but in any case it's a call for renewal.

Inside Sant'Egidio how do you deal with the problem of language, to avoid becoming a linguistic Babel?

In the church of Sant'Egidio we have simultaneous translation, which allows us to welcome many foreign groups. Our meetings are conducted in Italian, because we need a language to base the translations on. Since we're Italians we began with Italian; but today, in fact, at Sant'Egidio people speak French, German, and Flemish; a few speak Russian.

Latin?

No – and why should we?

For you personally, what is Islam?

That's a hard question. I can say that in the Italy I grew up in Islam didn't exist. It was a very distant image, almost confined to folklore. The case of Italy, in that sense, is different from France or Great Britain. Until not very long ago, there were no Muslim communities in Italy, and the ties with Islamic countries were tenuous. I would also say that the Italian republic neglected its traditional interest in Islam and the Arab world, which was, however, fairly vital from the end of the 19th century on, thanks to the country's Mediterranean ambitions. After the war the Italians were busy with other problems.

Certainly there have been some exceptions even in the Italian republic. I'm thinking of the petroleum politics of Enrico Mattei with the ENI (National Hydrocarbon Industry). As a historian, I've reviewed the initiatives for dialogue proposed by Giorgio La Pira, the mayor of Florence from 1951 to 1957 and from 1961 to 1966. He was a man convinced of the need to promote communication between the sons of Abraham: Jews, Christians, and Muslims. He kept up a very close friendship with Mohammed V, the King of Morocco, and with the Egyptian president Nasser. But he also had good contacts in Israel. Florence became a place for Mediterranean encounters.

During the years of my training, Islam was far away for Italians. Beginning in the '70s it came closer: the question of oil, the problem of the Middle East, the victory of Khomeini (we've forgotten how the Italian press once cheered for Iran's "green revolution"), a renewed culture, Muslim immigration, the exchanges on every level... Today Italians too discuss and debate about Islam. On the other hand, for Italy Islam is also close from a geographical point of view: the Balkans, Libya, the Maghreb. In 1994, after some polemics, the Great Mosque was opened in Rome.

And for the community?

Sant'Egidio began raising the question of Islam through the encounter with Muslim immigrants in Italy, with their faith and their problems. Some friendships developed between Muslims and Christians who were working for dialogue in the Islamic world. In brief we've begun to learn to know one another.

Nostra Aetate, Vatican II's declaration on the non-Christian religions, gave a powerful stimulus to dialogue with Islam. There was a period of enthusiasm, when new horizons seemed to be opening. The disciples of Louis Massignon, who for a long time had been hoping for a new Christian understanding of Islam, seized this occasion. I remember the Dominican priest, Father Georges C. Anawati and the conversations we had together in Cairo and elsewhere. He was a Cairene with a fine, even though highly concrete, reading of Islam.[4] Still we can't hide the fact that the enthusiasm felt by many Christians was followed by disappointment. Perhaps this was due to an overestimation of the capacity of a renewed Catholicism, now interested in dialogue, to influence Islam. Furthermore, some kinds of Muslim-Christian coexistence got into crisis situations, as in Lebanon or Cyprus. From the mid-1970s on, the actors in the Muslim-Christian dialogue have questioned themselves about the results. Many of them have the impression that the dialogue had no effect on the Muslim world. Now we find ourselves in a period that, forcing things a bit, I would call pessimistic, especially because of the appearance of Islamic fundamentalism. This doesn't take away the fact that there are some significant examples of dialogue with the Muslim world.

This enthusiasm corresponds to the period of the reception of *Nostra Aetate*. The disappointments are bound up with the absence of synchronism between the Christian world and the Muslim world. Christians were looking for dialogue at a time when Muslims were in a period of great ferment, in opposition to the West. The Muslim world was rediscovering its pride, first of all a nationalistic, then a religious pride. Ever since the 1960s, the dynamic of the Islamic world has been oriented toward a renewed sense of pride in itself. It's useful to recall the historical reasons for this, but the balance of the last few decades can't be drawn up in a simplistic fashion. Perhaps the dialogue was burdened by an "ecumenical" feeling that had no *raison d'être*. Did people want to reach agreements? Did they think they could totally modify Muslim attitudes? Perhaps. I think that in reality dialogue is a very long process; maybe it takes centuries.

Still, the dialogue has made it possible to know one another better and to put on the table some actual problems, such as that of the interlocutors. The mistake is often made of taking some high Muslim authority, a mufti for example, for the equivalent of a bishop. Sunni

Islam doesn't have a clergy, and we should know this. A mufti doesn't have the same representative quality as a bishop, and his statements can be rejected, even by a simple believer. At the same time there's no doubt that he *is* an authority in Islam. So that's how it is. Who, then, are the conversation-partners in the dialogue? At times one may get the idea that the real Muslim leaders are the politicians and not the religious personalities. There are also the intellectuals. And finally there is a spiritual Islam with which dialogue seems easier, because of a greater affinity in communication and expression than we find in other cases. But that's certainly not all of Islam. Then you can give a privileged status to dialogue with people at the grassroots, but you quickly realize that they too are conditioned by political and cultural frameworks. Islam "is a world", to borrow the expression of Émile Poulat. Perhaps many worlds.

As for myself, I think that no path of dialogue should be turned down, with the immigrant, with the poor Muslim, with the political leader, with the intellectual, with the Sufi. Yes, Islam *is* a world, and it can't be simplified; there's no one Islam, there are many. But isn't it the same, to a certain degree, for Christianity? If I said that Italian Christians are all sentimentalists while French Christians are rationalists, or that Spanish Christians are baroque, every one of us would be irritated by that sort of oversimplification. But we say much worse things about Islam; we abandon ourselves to incredible oversimplifications.

In fact, dialogue can't be a ten-year operation, at the end of which you're ready to roll out the balance sheet. It's a choice that involves a whole epoch, that gets played out over the span of a century and involves public opinion and the masses. That's the condition on which we believe in it. And then you have to acknowledge the different types of dialogue. There's a friendly, human dialogue; there's a religious dialogue. For example, I've been greatly moved by the sense of prayer that I've seen in Islam. On the other hand, as a Christian, I'm struck by everything that differentiates us from the Muslims on the question of law. Our culture and our faith don't imply this integral relationship between religion and civilization. Here we find one of the genetic characteristics of Christianity, which wasn't born as a state religion, but as a religion of persecuted communities, of people bearing witness. Christianity became a state religion much later. Islam developed in Medina, then in Mecca, as a religion of the city. Here we have a fundamental differentiating feature. For their part, Muslims have a hard time understanding Christianity; at times they fear our imperialism and at times, on the contrary, they don't understand the weakness of Christians.

We have to return to *Nostra Aetate*, which provides a basic orientation. We can't renounce dialogue, but it demands an "enduring patience". Dialogue is prompted by the dynamic nature of our faith; it's imposed by the geography of our people and their intertwining. My attitude starts out with these words in *Nostra Aetate*: "The Church views with respect the Muslims, who believe in only one God". Respect doesn't hide differences. Some fundamental concepts such as faith, revelation, prophets, freedom, the Word of God, have different meanings for Christians and Muslims. For this reason, some have talked about "ambiguity" in the dialogue, as if it were impossible to get any clarity at all on such slippery ground. That's the conclusion one might draw from more than one meeting.

We have to recognize the differences loyally, as John Paul II said in Casablanca: "There is a mystery here", he said, "on which God enlightens us, I am sure". And Monsignor Rossano,[5] who took part in the preparations for the Pope's trip to Morocco, noted how this phrase seemed to echo a phrase from the Qur'an: "We have ordained a law and assigned a path for each of you. Had God pleased, He could have made of you one community; but it is His wish to prove you by that which He has bestowed upon you. Vie with each other in good works, for to God you shall all return and He will resolve for you your differences" (Sura 5:48). Loyalty and clarity aren't opposed to the sense of mystery. Dialogue demands respect and clarity, not a polemical attitude, nor dissimulating one's own identity. And dialogue must deal not only with the different aspects of faith, but also with the whole sphere of human and social life. It's a matter of establishing a friendly contact between worlds with common or intersecting borders.

For me it's impossible not to recall, on this score, the great lesson of Cardinal Duval, the Archbishop of Algeria in the difficult years of the war (1954-62) and in the years of national independence. The cardinal wasn't an *arabisant*, but a solid Christian observer of the history of the Mediterranean. For him coexistence between Christians and Muslims was inevitable, but it demanded an attitude of dialogue and friendship. For this reason he considered Vatican II a providential event, even though the Council coincided with the end of the Christian presence in Algeria after the country won its independence. For Cardinal Duval dialogue had to pave the way to coexistence. I remember my last meeting with him, in his residence on the hill of Notre Dame d'Afrique, from which you can see all of Algiers, and at the foot of which lies the fundamentalist district of Bab el Oued. He said that he had never shared the sentimental illusions of some supporters of dialogue during the '60s and '70s. But, on the other hand, what other possibility is there beyond dialogue? Mutual ignorance? Collision? Nobody in Europe wants to relaunch the Crusades. No, the only choice left is patient, real, respectful dialogue. Here Christians have their responsibilities to carry out, and their role to play. It's necessary to open oneself – Cardinal Duval was convinced of that even in the final, very hard years – to a more far-reaching cultural cooperation.

How is all this lived at Sant'Egidio?

I have in mind some important moments of our dialogue with Islam. The first contacts were set up by some young people from the community with other young people, Muslims. Out of that grew genuine, touching friendships. These Muslims overcame the simplified image that Islamic countries too often get of the West. We spoke with Muslims who knew English or (a few of them) French and in any case had more than average openness. But in the Arab world there's a mass of people who live on the inside, without any kind of contacts with the western world, behind the walls of Arabic. What notion do they have of Christianity within that great non-communicating world? I have a personal memory of friendship with a young Algerian Muslim, who had been led, from these depths, to discover the nuances of the Christian world.

In 1989, for example, we organized a prayer session for peace in Warsaw on the occasion of the fiftieth anniversary of the outbreak of the Second World War; and we went on pilgrimage to Auschwitz. There were seven or eight Muslim leaders who didn't want to come, because they were convinced that Auschwitz was simply a Zionist mystification, an invention designed to make it easier to destroy the Palestinians. After the visit we had a long talk about it. They were deeply moved: "So it was true", they said. I have the impression that there are walls of ignorance. In this case dialogue performed a service to Judaism and, above all, to the truth. On the other hand, how can you understand the contemporary world while ignoring the reality of the *Shoah*? We've done a lot of work to set up opportunities for meeting between Jews, Muslims, and Christians. As recently as ten years ago it still wasn't possible, save as an exception. I sharply recall the harsh response that a grand mufti gave to Cardinal Martini when he suggested, around the mid-1980s, that the mufti talk with the Jews. But I've always felt it important to consider this meeting a priority, even if the problems that we all know continue to vex Jewish-Muslim relations. I still recall today the emotion in Malta in October 1991, when a call for peace in the Holy Land (it was at the beginning of the peace process) was signed by Jews, Christians, and Muslims. Among the signers was the grand mufti of Egypt, Tantawi, Rabbi Cohen of Haifa, Grand Rabbi Rosen of Bucharest, Sheik Sakouta of the Islamic League, the Greek Catholic Patriarch Maximos V Hakim, Archbishop Tessier of Algiers, and the Syrian-Orthodox metropolitan, Mar Gregorios Ibrahim.

The community of Sant'Egidio pursues dialogue with Islam on various levels; it would be pointless to furnish the details here (I'll only cite two working sessions with the *Rabita*, the world Islamic League, among many other meetings). I'm thinking of the visits by the religious leaders to Rome and of our visits to Muslim countries, from Egypt to Syria. The annual prayer for peace is a special occasion for dialogue and friendship. There have been meetings of every kind, including gatherings of young people. That way you create a habit of exchange and at the same time mutual familiarity. Thus some Muslims have acquired a better knowledge of Christianity and have overcome various prejudices. There's also our contribution toward solving some problems of these countries, which constitutes a surprising – and relevant – cultural sign in the Islamic world. Finally, not because it's less important, but because it may be the element with the weightiest consequences and the most diverse implications, there's our work of welcoming Muslim immigrants in Italy and Europe (Germany and Belgium, for example).

We had profound ties to a great Christian Arab, the Melchite metropolitan of Aleppo, Monsignor Neophytos Edelby who died in 1995. He was an advisor to the Melchite Patriarch Maximos IV Saigh at Vatican II, playing an important role, above all in the field of ecumenism.

He was a friend of the community; and he introduced us to the world of the Middle East and particularly to the Islamic world. He reminded us that, "Islam is a challenge flung at Christianity. It's a thorn, as Louis Massignon used to say, but it can also serve as a goad to collaboration among believers."

Yes, Islam *is* a challenge in many ways to the western world. But how to respond to that challenge? In the second half of the 20th century, as a result of Vatican II, we're drawing closer to an attitude that is both evangelical and realistic. That's why dialogue has to become consolidated in time. The moment hasn't arrived yet to draw up the balance sheet. Since we're Christians, we can't abandon ourselves to a sense of fear. Since I'm a European, I refuse to enter into a logic of fear that provokes dangerous reactions and the raising of new Iron Curtains or, rather, of new Maginot Lines. I'm convinced of the profound "strength" of our civilization, despite all its weaknesses.

Of Christian civilization?

Of European civilization, which is strong because it's complex. It's Christian and Greek, Latin, secular, Jewish, and even a little Muslim. It's above all Judeo-Christian and secular. In relations with Islam, the important thing is to overcome ignorance and stereotypes, knowing how to recognize yourself: this is fundamental. It's a field where the religions have a great deal to do and can achieve a great deal. The relations that we Christians have with society aren't the same as those of Muslims. They situate themselves in the world differently from Christians.

But before the Lord they have in common the attitude of believers who submit to the one God. Then, introducing Muslims to our Christian life, showing them young people who pray, people who believe, who live their social *jihad*, who are committed, who bear powerful witness – all this proves very useful for getting to know one another better, for combating the rather widespread notion in the Arab world that the Christian world is on its last legs.

One finds in Europe a discourse of fear about Islam, which runs contrary to the wish for dialogue and what dialogue implies, that is, trust in the future and optimism.

The fathers of dialogue, for example Massignon, were optimists. But exalting dialogue doesn't mean taking on an attitude of systematic or blind optimism, so much as being seriously, not superficially, realistic. There's no alternative to dialogue, to a serious, strong dialogue, charged with our identity. Why isn't there an alternative? Because it's imposed on us by moral and spiritual reasons, apart from geography. Otherwise what can you do? Build a wall? You have either the logic of bloc against bloc, or the logic of dialogue, as I've already said. In my view, rejecting dialogue is harmful and infantile, roughly equivalent to shaking the scarecrow of Islam. To achieve what? The organizing of a European Crusade? If we look carefully, we see that nobody doubts the existence of a clear and highly active will to develop economic relations with the Muslim world. That will is applied to wealth but not to dialogue, because dialogue is too demanding. There's a lot of hypocrisy here. We're told that we have to be afraid of Islam, while otherwise it's business as usual. And what are the political consequences of this sort of talk? What future is being imagined? None. Meanwhile people are being disinformed and, perhaps, thoroughly miseducated.

First of all, let's raise the issue of the relations between Christianity and Islam in Europe. What is the Islam that we find among us? Who are the Muslims around us? Islam in Europe is the Islam of the immigrants. In Italy dialogue means welcome, respect, witness to the value of a common life, a value based on secularity and freedom.

For example, dialogue means, to be quite concrete, extending the hours when our community dining hall is open during the month of Ramadan. Dialogue means before all else welcoming people, but also bearing witness to our civilization, which is humanistic, democratic, respectful and demanding of respect.

And in the Maghreb?

In the Maghreb the situation is difficult, particularly in Algeria. Unfortunately the Churches in these countries are foreign Churches. They were born as foreign Churches and perhaps they've remained such despite the choice of Cardinal Duval. Perhaps for this reason (but also because they're so tiny and because of the tragic conditions in Algeria) they work very hard at dialogue. But they're a great form of witness. I think especially of the life and death of the Trappist community of Notre Dame de l'Atlas, in Algeria, and of their prior, Father Christian de Chergé.

It's true, for dialogue you have to have at least two people. Dialogue seems possible in Europe. But can you establish it in countries where the Catholic Church is confined to a function of being a Church of foreigners, where it's impossible for a Muslim to convert to Christianity?

This is a very hard problem: the fundamental refusal to allow people to change religion, the prohibition, in some countries, against organizing worship for Christian immigrants, is really a poser. In our view this is unacceptable, something that by all means must be overcome. It's one more hurdle. Those who know how to move vigorously when they're in difficulties show a greater strength vis-à-vis their interlocutor, even if it's complicated to do so.

Besides, not all Christians are foreigners in the Arab world...

In the Maghreb there are foreign Churches with a colonialist past. But we mustn't forget that the Jewish communities, which have now disappeared from those lands, were once very important and weren't foreign. The Catholics, yes; they were Italians, French, Spanish, or Maltese. By contrast, the Jews were natives. This loss constitutes an important part of the debate. Then there are Christian Arabs in Egypt and the Middle East. Their contribution is still basic today and must remain alive. I'm thinking above all of the Coptic Church in Egypt, a popular force that has undergone profound restructuring. Sant'Egidio has always had a great friendship for the Christian communities of the Middle East. When Paul in his letters asks to be remembered to the saints of Jerusalem, to the mother Churches, I don't forget that our Church came from the East, *Lux ex Oriente*. We owe a considerable debt to our mothers, who now are ancient, and sometimes a little pale. These Eastern Churches are our mothers, despite their being internally divided, and even if the division among Christians arose in the East. The role of the Christian Arabs is strategic. They assure a presence of "secularity" in the Arab-Islamic world. Hence their presence in the heart of Islam is vital and irreplaceable.

Lebanon too has an essential importance, as John Paul II has said, because it constitutes for Christians a space of freedom, not just for them, but, I'd say, for the Middle East as a whole. I say this even though I believe that the region won't return to what it was yesterday; it's been too profoundly changed. The equilibrium of Lebanese society has been devastated. The war has destroyed a great dream. Perhaps Lebanon has to be reinvented. A spiritual renewal has to be achieved, perhaps starting out again from forgiveness and the need for the other. We have to work so that the different Muslim governments insure better living conditions for the religious minorities. Until recently Eastern Christians have been deluded concerning the positive role of the West. Sometimes I think this illusion still survives, perhaps in other regions, as in the Balkans. It's true that the West is part of the horizon of the Eastern Christians (some of them, at least), unlike that of the majority of Muslims. But the "protection" afforded eastern Christians by the West has been the source of confusion, illusion and exploitation.

The countries most favourable to Christians are the Syria of Hafez al-Assad and the Iraq of Saddam Hussein...

Yes, the Catholic Patriarch Bidawid makes the same point about Saddam's regime.

Iraq and Syria show how complex the situations are: it's not a question of democratic regimes, but of one-party dictatorships, by the Ba'ath. Still, there *is* a religious pluralism. It's tricky using western ideas here: can some secular values, such as equality, be exported to the Arab world? I think so, but it takes time. I'm proud to be able to say that in the Sant'Egidio platform, which was signed by the main parties of the Algerian opposition, from the secularists to the fundamentalists, religious pluralism has been recognized in Algeria. That wasn't a trivial fact. And I think it's important to observe that this guarantee isn't found in any Arab constitution.

We're involved in difficult situations, where dialogue is even more necessary. Dialogue has to be firm and strong. Our secret isn't military force or economic power. Instead, it seems more convincing to me to stress a generous moral force. In the case of Algeria we played this card. So when we get chided for taking certain initiatives in Algeria because we're Christians, I note that, on the contrary, Muslims don't find our behaviour perplexing. Rather, Muslims esteem a person who has the courage to call himself a believer. It's here that our strength lies; and you have to acknowledge that this strength is rather a weakness from the political or military standpoint.

Up until 1989 the press, and the intellectuals too, often

played on the subject of the fear of communism and the weakness of the West, as they said, to resist the pressure of the Soviet empire. Today communism seems to have been replaced by Islam, with the same arguments: the weakness of the western democracies, of Christianity in particular, in the face of an Islam described as monolithic and powerful.

I think your point about this process of transforming the "enemy" is true. We're witnessing a substitution of Islam for communism. In my opinion, this process is of the utmost importance. Some time ago the former secretary general of NATO, Willy Claes, argued along these same lines that NATO's defence system had to turn away from the East and toward the South, because the enemy now was Islamic fundamentalism. Strategically there's little ground for this, because the atomic threat, which has escaped the Kremlin's control, comes essentially from eastern Europe and the East in general. In a word, some people believe that there's a Cominform of the Muslim countries, that is, a Pope of Islam. He might be, for example, Hassan Tourabi, the leader of the Sudanese Muslim brotherhood, a man who has worked for the coming of an Islamic regime in his country.[6] And then they suspect the presence of "fifth columns" among the immigrants, who are assigned the role that once belonged to the communist parties, who were the fifth column of Moscow. The immigrants supposedly carry out this function on behalf of the "Islamic party". But this is to forget the formidable diversity of Islam as well as its frailties: for example, the condition of the Muslim woman, which can represent an opportunity both for Europe and for Islam.

But is there a fundamentalist threat, or is it just an invention of the western media?

The acts of violence and terrorism can't fail to disturb us. Fundamentalism is the dark terrain on which this threat grows. Fundamentalism often organizes and channels the reaction of a marginal world: I'm thinking of the students or the unemployed workers in the suburbs of Algiers. It can be an ideology for those whom Franz Fanon called the "wretched of the earth" and to whom he pointed out the path of revolution. Fundamentalism also becomes a defence of one's own identity vis-à-vis globalization and westernization. These processes have had more devastating effects in the South than in our countries. The title of a recent book, *Jihad vs. Mc World*,[7] and the arguments behind it, by Benjamin R. Barber efficiently sum up the issue, which is more or less "the holy war against globalization".

The term "fundamentalism" is often used, though a bit randomly, in the pages of newspapers. It's a reflex of fear and it encourages fear. But before stirring up fear the prudent thing would be to analyze the reality of fundamentalism, without leaving its interpretation to those prejudiced by the past or to vague feelings of discomfort. The notion of fundamentalism as a new threat presupposes the presence of a rigid ideology and an efficiently coordinated force enabling it to acquire the dimensions and strength to threaten the West. But the world of fundamentalism is complex, varied, and divided. *L'Atlas mondial de l'Islam activiste* reports this complex interweaving of elements that is often full of internal conflicts.

Is fundamentalism the beginning of the "clash of civilizations" that Samuel Huntington[8] has evoked as the inevitable destiny of history? In the face of fundamentalism, he argues, nothing can be done except to mount a police strategy to articulate and guarantee the security of the West. This position is also based on a reading of Islam as a religion inevitably dragged toward fundamentalism by its own internal logic. This reading strikes me as inclining too much towards the Catastrophe theory. In my opinion Olivier Roy is right when he maintains: "The debased form of Islam that we see in neofundamentalism is not a geostrategic factor. It will not unify the Muslim world; it will not change the balance of power in the Middle East. From Casablanca to Tashkent, the Islamic movements have taken on the framework of the existing States from which they adopt their mode of exercising power, their strategic claims, and their nationalism."[9]

In fact, differentiated national solutions can restore the real outlines of the Islamic problem. One very interesting case is the Jordan of King Hussein, where a special, democratic kind of experiment has been conducted with fundamentalism. In an intelligent study of democratization in the Islamic world, an Arab intellectual, Ghassan Salamé, has raised the issue of using the "democratic-electoral method" in the Islamic countries. It's not a question of putting an Enlightenment myth to the test, but rather of knowing whether elections and democracy are the only path for channelling the tensions and conflicts in a pluralistic society. Perhaps more work has to be done to divert the tensions into political struggle, as opposed to armed conflict or diffuse violence. The changing of governments has to be guaranteed by means of the ballot. The West, which has imposed an embryonic democracy on many African countries, ought vigorously to help this process along instead of being paralyzed by fear.

The fear of communism, then the fear of Islam, reveal that we have a mental pattern based on the demonization of the other. In my opinion, this is a sign of decadence. It's no accident that the parties of the far right, which in our civilization historically don't represent the forces of courage and generosity, are the ones that exploit the fear of Islam. The racist, xenophobic, Le Penist right doesn't stand for the open city, but for the village that closes itself off from the world. It's not the spirit of Rome nor Paris nor Milan nor Madrid. But it might be the spirit of the city's edge, of an edge that wants to be a village. It's not the spirit of a rich civilization that knows its own strength, but of a province that wants to shut itself off. This talk about the fear of Islam betrays a whole politics of fear. But you don't make politics based on fear. Or perhaps you do, but then it's a politics that contradicts itself, a tribal politics that I can't identify with.

The recourse to fear, and even to the notion of a conspiracy, returns at different moments in our history.

Yes, because it's a structural element of our political mentality. Fear gives rise to authoritarianism. Democracy isn't the child of fear, but of trust.

And of virtue as well...

Of trust and virtue, to be sure. American democracy, with its attention to checks and balances, rests on a certain wariness about possible temptations facing the individual, but also on an enormous confidence in the good that he or she can bring forth. Fascism, by contrast, is the result of fear and laziness; it's born out of a lack of trust in human beings: and then you have to find a "man on a white horse", an "anointed" of the Lord, to guide the masses.

Fear is an instinct. So then fascism is an instinct...

And democracy is reason. It's respect for the body of society in the plurality of its groups and their interests. It's the recognition of the human being as a person. Yes, to put it in a highly schematic style, democracy is reason and fascism is instinct. The question remaining is, what does it mean to defend and build democracy in a globalized world, dominated by "videocracy", while resisting the temptations of fundamentalism? Fundamentalism is a broader phenomenon than "Islamism" and traverses a great many cultural and religious worlds.

Can Christianity be at the same time a witness and a mediator? What are we to think of the way in which the Sant'Egidio initiative has been perceived in Algeria?

Sant'Egidio in Algeria is a collection of actions driven by one realization: it was impossible to ignore the Algerian tragedy, with its 300 to 500 deaths a week (to stick to bare, terrible numbers). People were too resigned to this situation. In 1994 in Assisi, during the Prayer for Peace, some Algerians asked me why we weren't doing something there as we had in Mozambique. Of course, it was impossible to repeat the same pattern as in Mozambique: the situation was different. But in November, 1994 we invited all the players in the crisis, including the government, to get together. We wanted to ask our Algerian neighbours how on earth their house had caught fire, and whether anything could be done about it. Many came and talked; and they asked to see us again to continue the dialogue.

We were driven by the conviction that there's no military solution to the conflict. To arrive at a political solution, you had to engage the fundamentalists in a common framework, at least those among them who, first of all, realized the futility of armed conflict. You had to conduct a dialogue with the different parties. The Algerian government reacted harshly at the end of our first meeting, declaring it a "non-event", and then starting up a campaign of what by European standards can only be defined as disinformation.

The government has organized many hostile demonstrations in Algeria. I can affirm – I say this in jest – that no saint has ever been as popular in Algeria as Sant'Egidio, not even St Augustine. Sant'Egidio has become a common word in the Algerian vocabulary; it's come to mean "dialogue". An Italian journalist wrote me that he saw graffiti on a wall saying, "Long Live Sant'Egidio", in other words, "Long live dialogue". Another journalist told me that people, the man and woman in the street, weren't familiar with the Rome platform, but for them Rome *means* dialogue.

144

Platform for a political and peaceful solution to the Algerian crisis

Today, January 13, 1995, the opposition parties in Algeria, gathered in Rome at the Community of Sant'Egidio, declare that:

Algeria today is living through a tragic, unprecedented trial.

More than thirty years after having paid a harsh price for its independence, the people have not been able to see realized the principles and all the objectives of November 1, 1954. They have gradually seen the fading away of all the hopes born after October 1988.

Today the Algerian people live in an atmosphere of terror never experienced before, oppressed by intolerable social and economic conditions. In this war without comprehensible contours: kidnappings, abductions, assassinations, systematic tortures, mutilations and reprisals have become the daily bread of the women and men of Algeria.

The consequences of the events of June 1991 and of the *coup d'état* of January 11, 1992, the interruption of the electoral process, the blocking of political activity, the dissolution of the FIS, the introduction of martial law, the repressive measures and the reactions to them – all have provoked a logic of conflict.

From that time on, the violence has not stopped increasing and spreading. The attempt by the authorities to create militias among the population seems to be an example of the remedy being worse than the disease. There are real threats of a civil war, and they have come to menace the physical integrity of the people, the unity of the country, and Algeria's national sovereignty.

A comprehensive, political, and equitable solution is urgently needed, so that other prospects may open up for a population that longs for peace, stability, and popular legitimacy.

Entirely on their own the authorities have initiated a false dialogue that has served to cloak unilateral decisions and the politics of the *fait accompli*.

Real negotiations remain the only way to arrive at a peaceful and democratic solution.

A. FRAMEWORK: VALUES AND PRINCIPLES

The participants bind themselves to a national contract, whose principles are the following (unless they are accepted no negotiations will be valid):

— The declaration of November 1, 1954: "The restoration of the Algerian State, the democratic and social sovereign power, within the framework of the principles of Islam" (art. 1).
— The rejection of violence to acquire or remain in power.
— The rejection of every dictatorship of whatever kind and the right of the people to defend their (freely) elected institutions.
— Respect for, and promotion of, the rights of the human person as enunciated by the Universal Declaration, the international pacts on the rights of man, the international convention against torture, made valid in legal documents.
— Respect for political change by means of universal suffrage.
— Respect for popular legitimacy. Freely elected institutions can be called into question only by the will of the people.
— The primacy of legitimate law.
— The guarantee of the basic freedoms, individual and collective, regardless of race, gender, (religious) confession, or language.
— The establishment of a multiparty system.
— Non-interference by the army in political affairs. The return to its constitutional responsibilities of safeguarding the unity and integrity of the nation's territory.
— The constitutive elements of the Algerian personality are Islam, Arab and Tamazight identity; the culture and the two languages that contribute to the development of that personality must find in this unifying framework

their place and their institutional advancement, without excluding or marginalizing anyone.

– The separation of the legislative, executive, and judicial powers.

B. MEASURES THAT MUST PRECEDE NEGOTIATIONS

1. The effective release of FIS leaders and all political prisoners. The leaders of the FIS must be guaranteed all the measures needed to allow them to gather freely among themselves and with all those whose participation is considered necessary for making decisions.
2. The opening of political space and the media. The cancelling of the decision to dissolve the FIS. The full reestablishment of the activities of all the parties.
3. The abolition of the measures banning and suspending journals, writings and books that have been introduced by citing a state of emergency.
4. The immediate, effective and verifiable cessation of the practice of torture.
5. The end of capital punishment, extrajudicial executions and reprisals against the civilian population.
6. The condemnation, and call for the end, of the harassment and attacks on civilians and foreigners, and of the destruction of public property.
7. The setting up of an independent commission to investigate the acts of violence and serious violations of human rights.

C. RE-ESTABLISHING PEACE

A new dynamic for peace implies a gradual, simultaneous, and negotiated process that includes:

– On the one hand, real measures of a thaw: closing of the security camps, the end of martial law and abrogation of emergency measures.

– On the other hand, an urgent and unambiguous call for the end of violent clashes. The women and men of Algeria hope for a rapid return of civil peace. The ways in which this commitment is applied will be determined by the two conflicting sides with the active participation of the other representative parties.

A similar dynamic demands the full and entire participation of the representative and political forces. These can contribute to the success of the process under way and insure the support of the population.

D. RETURN TO CONSTITUTIONAL LEGALITY

– The parties commit themselves to respecting the Constitution of February 23, 1989. Amendments can be made only by constitutional methods.

E. RETURN TO POPULAR SOVEREIGNTY

The parties present at the negotiations must define a transitional legitimacy by activating and monitoring the accords. For this reason they must set up a national Conference supplied with real jurisdiction, consisting of effective authority and representative political forces.
This Conference will define:

The temporary structure, the modalities and the duration of the transition period, which will be as short as possible, necessarily leading to free and open elections that will allow the people the full exercise of their sovereignty.

Freedom of information, free access to the means of information, and conditions for a free choice by the people must all be insured.

Respect for the results of this choice must be guaranteed.

F. GUARANTEES

All the sides present at the negotiations have the right to obtain reciprocal guarantees.

The parties, while keeping their autonomy to decide:

− are opposed to every interference in the internal affairs of Algeria;
− denounce *de facto* internationalization, the results of the politics of conflict promoted by the authorities;
− remain convinced that the solution of the crisis has to be exclusively the work of Algerians and has to be realized in Algeria;
− commit themselves to conducting an information campaign with the international community, aimed at making known the initiative of this platform and ensuring that it receives support;
− have decided to launch an international appeal to support the existence of a political and peaceful solution in Algeria;
− call upon the international community to show active solidarity with the Algerian people;
− have decided to maintain contacts among themselves with a view to consultations and permanent coordination/cooperation.

for the LADDH Abdenour ALI YAHIA
for the FLN Abdelhamid MEHRI
for the FFS Hocine AÏT AHMED
Ahmed DJEDDAI
for the FIS Rabah KEBIR
Anwar HADDAM
for the MDA Ahmed BEN BELLA
Khaled BENSMAIN
for the PT Louisa HANOUNE
for Ennahada Abdallah JABALLAH
for JMC Ahmed BEN MOHAMMED

In January, 1995 another meeting was held in Rome in which only the members of the opposition participated. This gave rise to the "Sant'Egidio Platform", a proposal for dialogue with the government designed as the beginning of a democratic transition and the escape from violence. The first result to flow from it was the insertion of the FIS into a coherent political framework with the other democratic and secular forces. An accord limited to the two extremes, the military and the fundamentalists, was certainly not desirable: it would have been a pact between "hawks", feared by many people and yet anything but unusual. At the end of a long negotiation the participants managed to create some unity in the Algerian opposition. In this way the FIS, no longer isolated, would enter into a process of internal maturation. Besides, the fundamentalist leaders know that a struggle to the bitter end will make the extremist and militarist factions emerge even more prominently in the Islamist movement. And so the necessary preliminaries were created for getting the FIS into a legal framework, alongside the other opposition parties, and for moving towards some sort of normalization of the Algerian crisis. In the Islamist movement, in recent years, and also thanks to the meetings in Rome, there have been notable developments and profound divisions with regard to the problem of violence.

The *coup d'état* in January 1992 wasn't just a response to the electoral success of the FIS by Algeria's "military society", which has controlled the government and the economy for more than thirty years. It was a complete rejection of the process of democratization, which had been deliberately chosen, for good or for ill, by President Chadli after 1988. The Rome Platform represented a political act of great importance: an attempt to relocate the process on political ground, by moving beyond a purely military logic. Despite the harshness of the government's reaction to the signatory parties, the military authorities have had to pay attention to the Platform.

The presidential elections from which Zeroual emerged the winner, in spite of the doubts that had been raised, represented a step in the direction of politics. The Platform pushed the Algerian military out of the lonely cage of the logic of conflict and forced even them to respond with a political act. With the Platform, politics rediscovered its primacy after three-and-a-half years of crisis. And that was its second result.

To be sure, the road to peace in Algeria is still a long one. We have to travel on the path of negotiations and of the revival of a normal democratic system. But experience has shown that we can't simply remain spectators. Losses in the Algerian civil war are now around 80,000 dead. There's a need for deeper reflection on this fact and for asking ourselves whether there isn't a middle way between repression and savage terrorism. This is something the international community has to think about.

Those who reject the peace platform point to two elements: foreign interference in internal Algerian affairs and clericalization. As for the "interference" in internal matters, I reject this accusation as an example of "Bulgarian language" – begging pardon of the Bulgarians, but it's a proverbial figure of speech – it was the Soviets who used to denounce as interference every initiative in favour of human rights in their empire. On the second point, I know some have said that this meeting in Rome was ambiguous, because it took place in the city of the Pope and hence represented a Catholic initiative. Another rebuke came from the Algerian bishops. But the charge doesn't seem well-founded to me: the organization of this meeting was a sign given by some Christians who showed that they wanted to work for peace. There certainly was no desire to humiliate Islam. Many groups in the Arab world viewed it positively, with astonishment and interest. Just look at the Arab press.

"The first meeting of the representatives of the FLN, the FIS, the FFS, of minor parties and various Algerian personalities, took place in Rome at the prompting of the Community of Sant'Egidio in November 1994, at the point when repression was reaching its zenith. The participants mean to bring Algeria out of chaos, to undertake real change by challenging once more the monopoly of power exercised by the army and its civilian connections, by preparing a co-management for the transition period... In their vision of things the return to peace will pass through a kind of regime of parties on the model of the French Fourth Republic, governing the balances between the formations and the personalities involved, without a 'man sent by Providence'. To achieve this the method is as important as the substance, and nothing appears more dangerous for the future than hasty elections in a country in ruins and overwhelmed by violence."

Extract from R. Leveau, *L'Algérie dans la guerre* (Brussels, 1995) pp. 127-128.

The dialogue that has been undertaken is risky, but it's built on concrete facts. Aït Ahmed, president of the FFS, told me that this meeting seemed to him the opposite sort of message to the one sent by the Gulf War. This time the West had promised dialogue and peace. In my opinion this is a sign of solidarity between Christians and Muslims, perhaps in a new phase of Islamic-Christian relations.[10]

This initiative came from Rome. Might it have come from France?

I don't know. Perhaps there's too much passion in the relations between France and Algeria. First of all, there's the passion arising from personal histories. There are people born in Algeria, people whose parents were *pieds noirs*, people related to those who've gone back to their homeland, people who are close to the Algerians. Algeria is not just a former "colony", it's also a part of France, or at least it's been thought of and experienced that way, even by some Algerians. When I listen to young Algerians, including fundamentalists, I notice that they talk about France with feelings that are anything but routine: they're inflamed, the way you talk about a close relative. And then, to tangle things up even more, there's the whole Algerian emigration to France.

Italy and Spain can do a great deal to help resolve the Algerian problem, but the keys to it lie in France. France can't pretend that Algeria is something like Switzerland. Neutrality isn't easy or possible, because when you find yourself actually involved, you have to take on your own responsibilities. Dialogue is the required path, because there's no possibility of victory in the field. France couldn't win the war in Algeria, even though in 1962 it had about half a million men facing a population of eight to nine million Algerians. Today there are twenty-seven million Algerians; and the Algerian army, which isn't the French army, can muster only 120,000 men on this front.

Under these conditions, in view of the impossibility of a military victory, the armed struggle does nothing but destroy many areas of society and radicalize the fundamentalists. Putting off dialogue is a serious mistake that can have more long-term consequences. France is often accused of this, and France certainly has things to answer for. But I don't think that we should isolate France – how could we? – or put the blame on it, or attribute to it mistakes that depend, in reality, on Algeria itself. There are, to be sure, French responsibilities; but there are others, and fundamental ones too, that belong to Algeria. The regimes of Boumedienne and Chadli weren't French but Algerian. I really have the sense that in the face of the Algerian problem France finds itself in a state of shock, aggravated by a widespread feeling of powerlessness. As if lying to themselves, many people try to believe that the problems have been resolved. We mustn't leave France alone on this issue: here we get back to the European question. Some actions have to be carried out jointly: Italy and Spain, Europe... not, of course, to interfere in Algerian affairs, but to back up the hopes for peace and the desire to get out of this terrible crisis.

Twice now you've mentioned the role of Italy and Spain. But is official action by governments desirable or even possible in the current phase? When you talk about Rome, in fact, when you cite the "Rome Accords", you're referring to a private initiative and not to intervention by the Ministry of Foreign Affairs.

This problem is very important and goes far beyond the question of Algeria. Italy (I mean the Italian government) has defended the idea of dialogue in Algeria. Of course, the Italian position isn't identical with the initiative of Sant'Egidio. We put ourselves on two sharply different levels. On some points I think that we've opened the road, but now the issue depends on the governments, and no longer on private initiatives. Still I think that we have to get out of an exclusively governmental concept of international relations. In fact – and not just today – many non-governmental structures have taken on an international weight: for example, in the case of Italy, Mattei's ENI (ENI is the Italian state-controlled oil company, currently undergoing privatization) has conducted its own foreign policy, hence the state monopoly in this field has already been cut into. One of the merits of Italian foreign policy is that it doesn't ignore this fact and often considers it one more opportunity. Again you could point to the initiatives of the PCI (Italian Communist Party) during the years 1960-1970, or to those of the mayor of Florence, La Pira. There is a notable synergy between public and private, in which we've found our place.

Did this synergy work well for Mozambique?

Yes, very well: the initiatives of Sant'Egidio blended very well with the action of the government.

The European Union has spread towards the North; tomorrow it will stretch out towards the East. Will this shift in the axis of Europe call into question again the role of Rome?

Rome is a very special city. Perhaps it isn't the "incredible city" that the 19th century German historian Gregorovius spoke of, but it certainly is special. It's the capital of Italy and at the same time a symbolic city: it's the only "sacred city" of the monotheistic religions that's located in a tranquil political democracy, in any event, outside of controversies, in the northern part of the world. Jerusalem, Mecca, and even Benares live within different frameworks. Rome is both a sacred city and a democratic city. The idea of a sacred city usually appears to contradict pluralism and democracy. But Rome is a sacred city *and* fully qualified to be the capital of a democratic, western state. When you go to Latin America and Africa, especially in Christian environments, and you say, "I come from Rome", people look at you sympathetically. Why? What does the name of Rome signify? What idea do they have of Rome in the world? Certainly an idea that doesn't totally match the reality; perhaps it's a slightly mythical idea. Because of the presence of the Holy See and Christian tradition, Rome is a headquarters for human and religious relations; these relations concern not only Catholics, but the ensemble of Christians and even non-Christians. Rome has significance even for the Copts of Egypt: and this is a fact of considerable importance. This city benefits from a fabric of exceptional richness; it's a double capital, with two diplomatic corps (one accredited to the government of Italy, the other with the Holy See), the FAO and a major foreign presence. This rich fabric is not always used as it could be.

With the arrival of tens of millions of pilgrims, the Jubilee of the year 2000 will provide the occasion for fresh reflection on Rome. There's a need for hotels, roads, parking; but above all there's a need for a new idea of Rome: a city that can't have the same meaning that it had in the days when the Pope never left, when you came to Rome to see him. Today we see the Pope all over Italy, in France, in Belgium, in the USA, on the Fiji Islands. Still, those who come to Rome for the Holy Year 2000, will come to see the Pope in Rome, that is, to see not just the Pope, but the pair, Pope-Rome. There's something to say and to ponder here. The Jubilee offers an opportunity to meditate on the meaning of Rome. We should elaborate as soon as possible a project with the civic and religious authorities, with the live forces of the city.

The Bishop of Rome often makes statements outside Rome and outside Europe. Is this because the Pope is taking note of a shift in the axis of Christianity outside his old historic lands? The same day that l'affaire Gaillot (Gaillot is a French bishop censured by the Vatican) broke out in France, John Paul II was in Manila. While the French media seized on that mediocre scandal, millions of persons were cheering the Pope at the other end of the planet. Two contrasting images, one next to the other: the old land of Christianity, now worn out, juxtaposed with new forces. How should we evaluate these shifts, which are charged in any case, like it or not, with consequences for European Christianity?

I agree, there's been a shifting of the Church toward the South. In reality it's a fair rebalancing. Yes, the Church has gone very much to the South, and the numbers of the faithful show it. The Popes have shifted the social question: up until John XXIII it was a European question, namely the proletariat; from Paul VI on it was transformed and became the question of relations between North and South. Today that's one of the essential points of the Church's social doctrine.

We have to remember that the Church isn't present everywhere: the great problem is Asia, where the Church hasn't succeeded in decisively penetrating beyond the Philippines, India, Vietnam, and South Korea. In Asia, it seems that communism has had a much stronger inculturation and has been more toughly rooted than in eastern Europe.

Since we're speaking about these topics, it strikes me as useful to call attention once again to the need for avoiding some preconceptions, such as a mystical vision of the South, where Christianity is supposedly pristine, whereas in the North it's old and corrupt. We often need to create these Manichaean pairs, which don't fit an increasingly more complex reality. It's true that I can't participate in a eucharistic liturgy in Mozambique or observe how the people pray there without being profoundly touched by it. The mass in this or that parish of Milan or Paris, by contrast, leaves me cold, while the mass in Beira moves me deeply. I remember going to Guatemala, in a little native village with an ancient church, consecrated, it was said, by Bartolomé de Las Casas himself. It was full of natives (the children were making their first communion), and their singing pierced your heart. But in Latin-American or African Christianity there are also weaknesses. I think we mustn't look for a "virgin" Christianity, but rather discover a young Christianity that's beginning to become established. Thus the cases of Rwanda and Burundi make us reflect on the weakness of Christianization there. We have to feel a great love for this young Christianity because many trials await it and it can unleash so many energies. One must note, at least, that without the Pope the Churches of the South would have had many more difficulties in freeing themselves from colonialism.

So we have here not a problem of North-South relations, but a problem of collegiality *cum Petro*, around the successor of Peter, which shifts the accent from the North toward the South. I owe this observation to Cardinal

157

Duval, the Archbishop of Algiers. During the synod of 1971, he was the one who said that the function of the Pope was to put an end to the colonialism of the hierarchy, but also to "financial colonialism"; because the potent finances of the northern Churches, while they can help a great deal, can on the other hand also control the southern Churches.

In any event I maintain that it's up to us to learn from the South. In the North, which in some ways really is tired, there's a witness to be grasped: the idea is not to imitate it, but to relocate ourselves, all of us, before the Gospel. Everyone has his or her culture, but the testimony of the South obliges us once again to face hard questions.

Has this re-balancing between North and South been accentuated with a Pope from the East?

This rebalancing already has a long history. It began with Benedict XV, and Paul VI gave it extra impetus. But, unquestionably, the Pope from the East has changed many things.

An acceleration?

You can speak of acceleration. John Paul II has put in higher relief some problems that will be solved only in the coming decades, such as the relationship between the ministry of the Bishop of Rome throughout the world and the government of the Church. He has strongly accentuated this itinerant ministry, which expresses itself in the form of a pilgrimage. In this way he has reinforced the ties with the bishops and the faithful. On the local, outlying level his speeches carry an extraordinary weight, something that perhaps we don't realize here in Italy because we hear so many of them. But I've been able to measure their impact in the course of various trips. In a number of countries, after all this time, people are still working today on his speeches, because, as they insist, "that's what the Pope said to our country". John Paul II also promotes a theology of the nations, according to which every Church, like every country, has its own vocation. We see him going through Poland, through Italy, through France. He's searching through every country for its role in the community of nations. Yes, there's no denying the fact that the universal character of the Bishop of Rome's ministry has been reinforced: on this point there's been a considerable acceleration. Projecting myself into the future, I ponder the next question, which is the relationship between this ministry and the government of the Church. Not that the ministry can be summed up in an external representation. But I believe that if after the Council we hadn't had a Pope like this one, we would have had great problems of unity, not so much because of the risk of schism, but because of the egocentric hovering over itself that can tempt every Church.

So there's a reinforcement of the role and of the image of Rome.

Now the question that arises is this: if we take into consideration the novel features brought in by the current pontificate, what becomes of Rome? What should the role of Rome be? I don't believe in any absolute division between the Roman curia and the local Church. Here in Rome, when he visits the parishes, the Pope says that he's the "Bishop of Rome". It's important: he doesn't present himself as "the Pope of the universal Church", but rather as "the Bishop of Rome".

Is the Roman Curia evolving toward an international bureaucracy? In fact I attach great significance to making it clear that I respect the bureaucracy; I surely don't want to say that what's bureaucratic isn't pastoral, because every effort needs to be supported, at a given moment, by a minimum of office work. The internationalization of the Curia effected by Paul VI was a timely measure; at one time the Curia was too Roman, then too Italian. But can it be transformed tomorrow into a sort of United Nations glass palace? I don't think that's either possible or advisable. The Curia can't become a kind of UN, because it's part of the *Ecclesia Romana* and has to maintain a particular ecclesial, human, and cultural bond with it. But there may be something of a risk that an international bureaucracy of the UN type will get formed. The process of internationalization has been a necessary fact, but now we have to begin to rethink Rome in this new context.

So, what's the responsibility of the Church of Rome alongside a Pope like John Paul II and his successors, whom I can't imagine not continuing on the same path? In my opinion, it must open itself still more to universality; and the Jubilee of the year 2000 will be the crucial test. For example, what does "welcome" mean? We'll have to explore all the theological density and concrete implications of the welcome. The world of the Vatican that came out of the trauma of 1870 (crystallizing in 1929 on the border of the two states, with the Vatican institutions on one side, and secular Catholic Rome on the other) is gone now. All this has to be rethought, with respect to the freedom of the Holy See and the secularity of the State: we need an "urban" and ecclesial imagination to rethink Rome. It's not enough to treat the city like any old diocese, otherwise the Holy Year will be a failure. So the problem arises of coherence between the role of the Pope and the role of Rome in the third millennium.

To organize the welcome in Rome, the civic authorities and the State have their responsibilities too.

Certainly it *is* a responsibility of the State and of the civic authorities, but that's limited to organizing things; it doesn't concern the sense that will be given to the welcome. Certainly, a farsighted administration can try to locate this rethinking of the city within a role it believes it can play in the international concert. I have the feeling that the topic of the Holy Year has become very important. Everybody's ready to invest in it, however late in the day. But we should also explain what our project consists of. In this sense the document by John Paul II, *Tertio millennio adveniente* (1994) is extremely important. The Pope calls for an in-depth revision of the life and history of the Churches. He writes: "The Holy Gate of the Jubilee of 2000 will have to be symbolically larger than in the preceding ones, because humanity, having arrived at that goal, will leave behind it not just a century but a millennium. It is well that the Church enter upon this event with a clear consciousness of what it has experienced in the course of the last ten centuries. It cannot cross the threshold of the new millennium without pressing its children to purify themselves..." But the Holy Year has to be the occasion for rethinking the Church of Rome at the dawn of the new millennium. So it's worthwhile to reflect on the fact that the Orthodox accept that a local Church has a primatial role to play. In this sense John Paul II has opened very important paths of reflection on the ecclesial and human level.

The question of what sort of welcome there should be on the occasion of the Holy Year reminds us that Europe finds itself facing the problem of welcome to the foreigner, to the foreigner of another race, let alone another religion. It's the problem of immigration, which is no longer an internal current in Europe as it was at the beginning of this century with the Italians in Germany or in Switzerland, or the Portuguese in France. In Italy they talk about "extra-communitarians", even though perhaps one should more correctly just say "immigrants". It's the fact (or problem?) of immigration as an "opportunity" or a "misfortune" for Europe, now that it's become one of the stakes in the game of the electoral debate. Reflection on this serious question strikes me as having occupied for some time now the agenda of the community of Sant'Egidio, which before all else has worked to help the poor. Currently many of the poor are immigrants. Is this an opportunity, then? Is it a danger? Instead of improving, the debate seems to have turned harsher and more difficult than ten years ago.

That's true. At a certain point in the 1980s at Sant'Egidio we realized that the immigrants were the new poor. Not the only ones, but perhaps the most numerous. And unexpected.[11] The parable of the Good Samaritan teaches us that the poor person isn't the one I met thirty years ago, but that we have to continue to be Samaritans, "to become neighbours", because the poor are changing. Today poverty is represented by the old, by the homeless, by people with AIDS, by foreigners, by refugees... In the beginning, for Sant'Egidio, the poor were children without education, or the old, the people who lived in huts. Today there's a large urban underclass that very often has the face of foreigners, those who've been given the ugly name of "extracommunitarians".

In this regard you've got to make some distinctions, because you can't treat immigration as a uniform European problem. France, for example, has its own history of immigration, which is already old, tied in with its colonial past. We must never forget that the colonial powers have a responsibility in this area, and that there are some accounts that come due thirty or fifty years afterwards.

Can the same be said of Great Britain?

Great Britain is in a situation similar to France's. Germany isn't; the strong presence there of immigrants is not due just to its own colonial history, but to important needs of the industrial work force and the boost provided by the Turks.

For Italy immigration is a more recent fact than for France and Germany. When we were children and we met an non-European on the streets, we looked at him with curiosity. This would happen in Rome not very long ago, not to speak of the provinces. In the provinces seeing an Indian with a turban was like going to the movies. Arabs made us dream mythical things: they were Saudi emirs; the Muslims were the Shah of Iran with Soraya. Or they were caricatures, something out of cartoons.

The case of Italy in Europe has its own special features. We had some provisions in the immigration law that left open many breaches. I'm among those who believe that Italy can still accept a certain number of immigrants, given that they make up less than 2% of the population and that Italy remains among the last three countries in Europe for the numbers it opens its doors to, while having an income and population not much smaller than France, Great Britain, or Germany. It won't be long before we begin to feel the impact from the lack of immigrants admitted into Italian society and the economy. There's room in Italy; and among our immigrants we have some components – from eastern Europe – that are non-Muslims and easier to integrate. We also have many Ethiopians and Eritreans; they come here because of our colonial history (and that history isn't a very pure one, either). We absolved ourselves of our African imperialism, while presenting France and England as harsh colonial powers. In general the Italians considered their worst national defect in this area the attention they paid to women of colour. In reality our colonial history is also made up of ferocious acts of repression: the conquest of Ethiopia was a barbaric enterprise, because of its methods, because of the use of poison gas, because of its objective, which was the destruction of an independent State, and of ancient traditions, which happened to be Christian. Our colonial history, then, is no better or worse than that of other European countries. It's perhaps just as mean-spirited, and only on a smaller scale than others'; but we too have heavy colonial responsibilities.[12]

Looking to the South, we have today a Christian

immigration coming from Eritrea, Ethiopia, and from Egypt too. In Rome there are 5,000 Egyptian Copts, to whom Sant'Egidio has loaned a church to celebrate the liturgy for the last eight years. In fact, immigration has become quite diversified; and the one kind that may seem hard to integrate is the Muslim immigration from the Maghreb. This is the problem, but it concerns only a very small group. In Italy the current difficulties – and a lot of wealth for the labour market – stem from the eastern European and, more particularly, the Albanian immigrants. Moreover this is the result of our TV "preaching" for many years in that country and of their collective desperation vis-à-vis the crisis of the State. Albanians have gotten the image of a country that's extraordinarily attractive and incredibly close, so they want to come here. They feel irresistibly fascinated and attracted by Italy.

There's a long history between Italy and Albania.

It's a quasi-colonial history. In recent years because of the changed visa situation the prevailing immigration has come from the East: Romanians, Poles, etc. They would like to be seasonal workers, though currently that's not how it works out. But I challenge the notion that, unlike immigration from the South, immigration from eastern Europe is acceptable because it's more easily integrated. There's an immigration from the South, from Africa, especially from Ethiopia, that can be perfectly well integrated into Italy. There are Ethiopian and Eritrean families that have meshed very well with us. I'm convinced that a civilized European country – however many difficulties it might have or think it has – must keep a door open to immigration. Still, I'm not totally in favour of endless Albanian immigration. In fact, while we Italians, as Italians, will never be able to resolve the problems of Ethiopia or the Maghreb, and while through this hospitality we can do positive things for them and for ourselves, with Albania it's different. We have to commit ourselves deeply, over there, to resolving the difficulties of Albania and thus to avoid the departure of a part of its population. It can be done there. The recent crisis of Albania shows how the Albanians have lost confidence in a common future. The logic of the clan has returned – as I said already – and people have reached back for their rifles. The problem today is to restore trust to the people of this country: in the government, in a common destiny, in a future of employment for themselves and for their children. We have to effect a reconciliation between North and South, between the parties. It's a challenge for Italy and Europe. But to return to the subject of immigration, we have to give separate consideration to politically motivated immigration. We've had some incredible situations in Italy, where Kurds, even minors, have been expelled. Most recently this has involved families of gypsies, living in Rome for many years, with minors born in Italy. Now our republican constitution obliges Italy to provide asylum for refugees, for people undergoing political persecution in their own countries. We used to be a place of refuge for the communist countries, but what's happening now? It seems to me that not renouncing our existence as a land of asylum is a matter of national identity and dignity. We can't accept limits on the right of exile.

The problem of immigration is very difficult; it has European and worldwide dimensions. In France it's more tragic than in Italy. Many people there suffer from a problem of identity: what does it mean to be Algerian, to be French, to be Muslim? Hysterical reactions have also been recorded, along with some attempts to exploit them. Are we looking at an invasion? I believe that we have to admit frankly, there have always been non-destructive invasions: I believe in the profound strength of our society, which has a considerable capacity for assimilation. Women immigrants play an important role in favour of assimilation, given what we say about work and feminine dignity. In that sense I think how counterproductive for Italy is its proverbial slowness in issuing permits for reuniting families.

In a debate with a person who maintained that Islamic immigration represented the peaceful conquest of the West by the Crescent, I said I was more "nationalistic" than he was, because I had full confidence in our civilization. We don't need the language of fear. In that respect our politicians are making a grave mistake. They follow up, they adopt the references to fear by the extreme right. The theorem is a familiar one: people are afraid of immigration, so let's chase the immigrants out. In my opinion, we have to act intelligently, by anticipating things, by keeping watch so as to forestall the situations of crisis and to resolve the problems of the immigrants with the help of a strong social policy. We have to insist on certain values; we have to teach them. If we don't do this, the expulsion of a hundred or so immigrants will not, to be sure, change our electoral configuration. Fear and the wish for scapegoats in moments of social trouble and an identity crisis, or in a state of transition, are hard to repress. And it's clear that at this point in time Italians are living through a phase of discomfort because of the sacrifices required by the reorganization of the economy; they're uncertain about their future, about jobs and pensions. There's a malaise. But that's a different problem. In my opinion, there's no threshold up to which it's good to pursue the feelings of fear and its violent consequences, so that beyond it they will disappear. Fear is a minority phenomenon; it would be disastrous to chase after it, thereby legitimizing it. That way the far right, instead, imposes its game and its language on us.

Let me take an Italian example I'm familiar with. In Apulia, whose ports see a certain number of refugees coming in, some politicians have shouted, "It's an invasion!" A friend of mine, Monsignor Cacucci, the Archbishop of Otranto, on the very heel of Italy's boot, has told me how many inhabitants of the country, as a whole, are showing generosity to Albanian immigrants.

They welcome a great number of them into their homes. The Archbishop talks about *carabinieri* who, after capturing at night some families who arrived clandestinely, took them to their own homes. We have to support this kind of attitude.

To some extent this is a crisis in our national identity: until recently we identified with political parties (we were Communists or Catholics or Socialists) rather than with our country, forgetting that our identity is an Italian identity. It seems to me that we've gone through a process fairly unique in Europe: we used to remember that we were Italians only when we went abroad and on the basis of certain elements, such as cuisine or the national soccer team. Today the rediscovery of Italian identity is passing through a stage not of closure but of openness. It's also a more profound reply to the thrusts of separatism. If we accept a narrow defence of our own interests, even the response to associationism becomes soft and weak. Also because then associationism is more consistent in sanctifying the cult of individual or group self-interest. I mean that we have to try to build a new, open identity. This imposes on us the obligation to speak in an eminently political way not based on emotion and instincts.

I continue to have confidence in our strength to integrate newcomers. The walls of confusion that some recent legislative measures have wanted to erect thanks to uncertainties in the law don't help. To be sure, I don't think that everything can be resolved in a primitive fashion, but I also have confidence in the capacity of Italian society to assimilate those who come here driven by necessity, and to respond to our economic needs. I found Duroselle's book on the "invasions" an acute analysis. The great French scholar asks: "Are human migrations an opportunity or a calamity?" I share his conclusion: "Assimilation, integration, fusion, depend on us, and on them (the immigrants). But we are the ones who must encourage them, because we are the model of the

Frenchmen they want to become. For all those who want to become French we are the model. All those who wish to set up two weights and two measures have to know that they are in danger of massacring French culture. Speaking for myself, in the evening of my life, I continue to believe that we will save it."[13] This confidence can inspire intelligent politics in Italy and elsewhere. It's not a question of fatalism as we confront an invasion; rather, it would seem to me to be a way of governing this process, instead of letting it be governed by chance or by hysterical reactions.

What should we say to the countries of eastern Europe that have liberated themselves from communism and are knocking at the door of the European Union, which they consider a sort of paradise?

On September 1, 1989 I was in Warsaw, in Castle Square, to celebrate the fiftieth anniversary of the Second World War with the Prayer for Peace organized by Sant'Egidio and the Church of Warsaw. There was a palpable atmosphere of anguish. I had never felt so strongly how much the memories of World War II were still alive in people. The pain, the recollections, the hopes were expressed with an extraordinary tactile effect. For me it was a deep and moving contact with the world of the East, in a moment of transition. I recall Tadeusz Mazowiecki, who had just been named prime minister, a refined man, attentive to the human side of things. There was General Jaruzelski, and there was Cardinal Glemp: along with us he had organized that event and that memorial in a new way – with an openness to the world religions and to reconciliation – in the centre of Poland, while playing a mediating role in that country's transition.

Despite the terrible memories of the war, all of this was like a new springtime. In reality, these people, who heroically freed themselves on their own, are now having a new experience of consumerism and nationalism. It's normal, perhaps. I don't share the prevailing judgement by a western Europe that believes itself superior to its neighbours. At the same time I have the impression that the past can't be thrown away completely. For example, meeting young Ukrainians and Russians, I've discovered their solid cultural and intellectual formation that, even with its well-known ideological dead ends, shows to what extent a part of the Soviet educational system still works. I mean simply, as is obvious but not commonly recognized, that we can't tell them: "You were completely wrong". Otherwise they'd have to begin from zero, without roots. So many decades of history weren't just one gloomy parenthesis. Now in every people there's an irrepressible need for roots and for trust. These are two absolutely fundamental necessities.

I continue to feel shaken by the terrible poverty that I found in those countries. African poverty is very harsh, but how frightening is the poverty of old people in Moscow, without any income, forced to live between walls where even grass won't grow, where there isn't a tree to pick fruit from, with no family, with no solidarity, completely alone. Life expectancy has noticeably dropped in the countries of the former Soviet Union, and suicides among old people in the cities have risen terribly. All this is not without significance. It's horrible. So, what's the mission of Christianity in these countries, particularly Russia and Ukraine? It's not a question of stirring up the rivalries between Catholics and Orthodox, but of asking what Christianity means: rediscovering roots, but also initiating a new mission, while the Orthodox Church is confronting the proselytism of the sects, whose spread causes it great concern.

But this isn't a problem specific to eastern Europe?

There's a fine document by the Holy See according to which the sects are expanding because they respond to a need for warmth that isn't being met in our Church.[14]

This is true. I made the same observation in Mozambique where, after the end of the war, the Churches, which had been strong during the troubles, didn't come forward in a collective effort: it seems to me that in building life in peacetime they couldn't muster anything like their earlier strength. Thus in Maputo some of the movie houses in the city were bought up by a Brazilian church-sect that's making a name for itself. In Guatemala you can't help being impressed by the number of sects in the capital itself, Guatemala City. We're facing a challenge that we ought to think about. We have to transform our churches into places of human warmth, into family communities. I'm not talking about giving in to sentimentalism.

On the contrary, sentimentalism is serenely growing in Churches that don't succeed in addressing all of life; they're blocked by their institutional structure, by ritual and habituation to social roles, both old and new. And along with sentimentalism grows an untroubled coexistence with Christian references, horoscopes, and not-so-occasional recourse to magic: that's what emerges in Rome itself from a recent national study of religious behaviour.

But there's another problem, a political one. The Church, whether Catholic or Orthodox, can't be manipulated, as happens with the sects, by the authorities, whether public or hidden. At bottom, the sects really are "religion as the opium of the people". They offer a religious life without civic or cultural dignity. Between the sects and the experience of the Church there's the same difference that exists between prostitution and marriage.

Eastern Europe means countries with a history that is only too tragic, whose symbol remains the genocide of the Jews at Auschwitz. For you is the Holocaust really the expression of God's silence?

Yes, that's how I feel about it when I think of a passage in the Gospel of Matthew: "If you have faith as a grain of mustard seed, you will say to this mountain, 'Move from here to there', and it will move; and nothing will be impossible to you" (Mt 17:20). Prayer said with faith moves mountains and works cures. But at Birkenau, Dachau, Mauthausen, at Risiera San Sabba in Italy, what happened?

At Auschwitz you feel the descent into hell: never had humanity sunk so low, so deeply towards hell; and the great majority sent there belonged to the Jewish people. There you realize the solidarity owed to the Jews, not just because they are "our elder brothers", but because they've suffered in such a way that each pang of anguish endured by a Jew today touches us personally. At Auschwitz I understood the silence of God; and it seems to me that I also perceived the manner in which the Jewish people perceive it. I felt the philosophical and emotional temptation to think of a powerless and hence impassive God. Still, I believe that reading Scripture frees us from a similar temptation. But at Auschwitz it's hard to say, "God is great, God is powerful". It's really the descent into hell through the incredible machine of annihilation assembled by the Nazis. It's a modern machine, plugged into medicine, industry, sociology, psychology, all sorts of organizations. But it's a machine that destroys, that has destroyed, the most diverse human beings, the Jews, the gypsies, the handicapped, its opponents, the homosexuals, the communists. And a large part of Polish society. A terrible mechanism. This is how far the monstrousness of modernity can go. Modernity without a soul, or with only the soul of dominion, individual or collective. For the fiftieth anniversary of the end of the Second World War John Paul II wrote: "Auschwitz, alongside so many concentration camps, remains *the tragically eloquent symbol of the consequences of totalitarianism*. Pilgrimage to these places with the memory and with the heart, on this fiftieth anniversary, is a duty... From this sort of meditation questions flow that humanity cannot fail to ask itself.

171

Why did they descend to such a point of annihilation of human beings and peoples?"

Do Christians have a responsibility for the Holocaust?

The letter of John Paul II on the end of the Second World War, in my opinion, is important; it also goes a long way towards answering your question, although the text hasn't been sufficiently noticed.[15] He underlines the scandal that the Holocaust should have taken place in Christian Europe, in countries with a Christian culture. In the face of this and of World War II we have to acknowledge that there's a weakness in Christianity. It can't be reduced to the diplomatic weakness of a Pope like Pius XII; it has to do with a vacuum in education, in evangelization, in history. If we had loved and respected the Jews better, what happened would not have occurred. This is true for Poland, for Germany, for Italy, for all our European countries. The mistakes, the responsibilities are profound, but not accidental. They don't depend purely on this or that specific decision. The responsibilities also have to be looked for in secular culture – there is in fact a secular anti-Semitism – as well as in the policies of the United States and of Great Britain, which closed the doors to Jewish emigration to Palestine. And there are many others. There's the terrible question mark hanging over many German Christians, Catholics and Protestants, along with the extraordinary witness of others, starting with Bonhoeffer. I don't say this to dilute the responsibility of Christians but to grasp better the weakness of Europe and the world in the face of the *Shoah*.

In view of such a horrible war we were really, all of us, defeated, even those who were victorious on the military level. We are all implicated to some extent. In that sense I share, and I feel myself obliged to share profoundly, the sufferings of the people of Israel. I understand the Jews' demand to benefit from the security of a Jewish state. They've lived through too many harsh experiences.

I also have to say that I feel a great friendship for the Palestinian people, doubtless one of the greatest Arab peoples. And I don't feel that this double friendship is contradictory. I hold out hope for peace; we have to have courage and trust in peace. There can be moments of discouragement, but trust is a question of time and continuity. This is the crucial point of the future in the Middle East. Establishing trust – *that's* the most important and difficult task.

Next year in Jerusalem?

For us at Sant'Egidio, at least since the beginning of the '80s, the experience of the Holy Land and of Jerusalem has been and is crucial, even just from the standpoint of familiarity with the Scriptures, with the Gospel. Jerusalem is a point of decisive reference, a centre of unity in the heart of the conflict. The three monotheistic religions are gathered together in Jerusalem, and there all three reveal their antagonism and their mysterious common destiny.

The Holy Sepulchre too is highly symbolic. In general those who visit there go away scandalized by the divisions among Christians: Catholics, Armenians, Orthodox, Ethiopians, Copts, Syrians all behave like hostile brothers. I'm not a stranger to this immediate response. But at the same time I have thought that paradoxically the death and resurrection of Christ succeeds in bringing all the Christian confessions, despite the mistrust and the conflict, to live together. It's an extraordinarily attractive force. Ultimately only the one Christian ecumenical church is there. There's no concelebration, but they share the same living quarters. Thus Jerusalem appears as the place where the clashes become even more tangled: there we find together factors of unity and factors of conflict among the Christian confessions and among the three great religions of the Book. At Jerusalem you can gauge better how much of the road remains to be covered.

And then there's historical Jerusalem, the new Jerusalem: is it Jewish? Palestinian? How to organize the participation of all groups in the reality and the vocation to unity that is the vocation of Jerusalem, when the Christian part has diminished almost to the point of disappearing, leaving the Jews and the Muslims face to face?

We're not thinking of opening a community in Jerusalem. If we were a religious community, we might consider it, but that's not what we are. Still, in recent years we've gained a great familiarity with Jerusalem. When you go there and stay for a while, it's a little like examining the back of the carpet: you see the unity and you measure the distance separating us from it.

And the prayer for peace in Jerusalem?

After having announced it twice, we managed to arrange an ecumenical encounter at the end of August, 1995. It was carried out in a way that was discreet, as befits the situation of the Holy City, but in a profound and lofty way too. Many kinds of opposition intersected; we had to keep in mind the contrasts in sensibility, the mistrust, the specific problems. We chose a place within the walls of the Old City belonging to the Armenian patriarchate. Here for two days Christians, Jews, and Muslims met. They talked and listened. The topics were the Holy City and Abraham in the three traditions. There was no lack of debate between Yossi Beilin and Feisal Husseini on the political future of Jerusalem. There were Orthodox, Protestants, and Catholics, Jews from Jerusalem and the Diaspora, Palestinian and foreign Muslims. There weren't a lot of people, but they created an atmosphere of seeking. Finally, in the garden of the Armenian patriarchate we planted three olive trees, symbols of the way the three religions are rooted in Jerusalem, the one next to the others in the same land. It's a little and a lot. The difficulties we had to overcome to get to this meeting show me that a lot, a very great deal, was achieved. At any rate it's a symbol, profound and strong, that can be referred to by anyone who has peace and coexistence in his or her heart.

Affirming the universal vocation of Jerusalem means helping peace, reaffirming that its future isn't expressed only by the national destinies. It was the first time, in the long history of Jerusalem, that the three great religions met peacefully in the enclosure of its storied walls with such distinguished representatives.

NOTES

1   Paris, 1949.
2   Maximos of Sardi, *Le patriarcat oecuménique dans l'Église orthodoxe* (Paris, 1975) p. 378. The problem of the jurisprudence of the various Orthodox national Churches in the diaspora is later than the one pointed out at the Council of 1872.
3   Oscar Cullmann, *L'unità attraverso la diversità* (Brescia, 1987) and *Le vie dell'unità* (Brescia, 1994).
4   Father Anawati was born in Cairo in 1905 and died in 1994. He entered the Dominicans in the '30s, and was one of the great masters of Christian-Muslim dialogue, as well as a great expert on Islamic thought and culture.
5   On this point see the Community of Sant'Egidio, *Cristianesimo e Islam* (Brescia, 1990).
6   Even if he doesn't have any official position, he seems to be the strong man in the Sudanese power struggle. See A. El-Affendi, *Tourabi's Revolution* (London, 1991).
7   B. R. Barber, *Jihad vs. Mc World* (Times book, New York, 1995).
8   S. P. Huntington, "Clash of Civilizations?" in *Foreign Affairs*, Summer 1993, pp. 24-49.
9   The quotations are taken from A. Riccardi, "Scacco in tre mosse per il '68 islamico. Come rispondere al fondamentalismo", in *Liberal* 1/1995, 66-70; *Foi et Développement* (Centre Lebret, June-July 1995) pp. 4-8.
10 The history of the difficult attempt to find a political, non-violent escape from the Algerian situation is reconstructed, up to our days, in M. Impagliazzo-M. Giro, *Algeria in ostaggio, Tra esercito e fondamentalismo, storia di una pace difficile* (Milan: Guerini e Associati, 1997).
11 Cf. *Stranieri nostri fratelli* and *L'ospite inatteso*, two volumes edited by the Community of Sant'Egidio in the series "Cieli aperti", from the Morcelliana publishing house.

12 See the Community of Sant'Egidio, *Immigrazione, razzismo e futuro* (Padua, 1990).

13 J.-B. Duroselle, *L'invasion* (Paris, 1992) p. 219.

14 This document comes from the Secretariat for Christian Unity, the Secretariat for Non-Christians, and the Pontifical Council for Culture, *I fenomeni delle sette o nuovi movimenti religiosi*, May 7, 1986.

15 *Message of the Holy Father Pope John Paul II on the Fiftieth Anniversary of the End of the Second World War in Europe* (Vatican City, 1995) p. 7.

CHAPTER FIVE
History and the Present

Sant'Egidio has never taken you away from your profession as a historian. In what sense has the community nurtured your thinking and guided your action? What link is there between historical research and civic commitment?

That's a hard question. The link between my commitment to Sant'Egidio and my work as a historian is found in my lived experience, it's in myself. They're two complementary activities, it's my life. But you also have to distinguish. Naturally I find myself facing immediate problems that put questions to the historian; it also happens that the results of historical research lead to questioning society today or widening one's horizons. I like the remark attributed to Fernand Braudel and E.C. Carr: "The present illumines the past, and the past illumines the present". It's just a quip, but I've found it close to the truth. In fact, I don't think that history is the *magistra vitae* (teacher or mistress of life) because, among other reasons, each person and every generation have their own responsibilities. Still, history opens up horizons that help us to understand the complexity of things and place them in proportion.

You've specialized in religious history and have done a lot of work on the history of the Papacy in the contemporary era.

I've also written a book about bourgeois Catholicism in France in the 1800s and about Monsignor Maret, a French bishop little known among us. The latter book was important for me: it allowed me to understand the religious history of contemporary France, which was forged mainly in Paris. In my view, Paris and France are for the Catholic Church the first laboratory where the relationship with modernity was put to the test. In no other great city did Catholicism have such a confrontation with the modern world. In London, Berlin, and Moscow Catholicism was largely a minority religion; and in Italy at that time there were no "modern" cities like Paris. I think of the great figures who were Archbishops of Paris, Monsignor Affre, Monsignor Sibour, Monsignor Darboy, who encountered modernity in the course of their pastoral mission, in the various appearances that it assumed: the working class, secularity, the bourgeoisie, freedom. I can't forget that in Paris the Catholic Church very quickly met "secularization" in the modern sense of the word, not only the secularization of the bourgeoisie, but also that of the working class. "Religion is lost in Paris...", a parish vicar charged in a letter to Archbishop Sibour in 1849.[1] For this reason the history of the Church in France has always deeply interested me. In Paris there is the issue of the worker-priests, which was launched by the question that Godin asked of Daniel: *France pays de mission?* ("Is France a missionary country?") It was in France that the clash between Catholicism and modernity took place, in all its complexity. The cycle that opened with the French Revolution closes with Vatican II, with new language about the world and to the world.

In my research I've concentrated, in turn, on the Church of Rome and the papacy in the 20th century. *Roma, "città sacra"?* (*Rome – a "Sacred City"?*), which I published in 1979, came out of a problem of which I had personal experience. I asked myself about the relations between the local Church and the Pope, and between the Church and civil society. But one historical work calls forth another; one book often contains some elements of its sequel.[2] Rome led me to study the papacy in the 20th century, above all Pius XII. Then I worked on the characteristics of Italian Catholicism. After that I was driven to extend my research into the relations between Christianity, Judaism, and Islam in the 19th and 20th centuries.[3] I recall spending a summer in the archives of the French Ministry of Foreign Affairs, on the Quai d'Orsay, to study the reports of the ambassadors of France in the Mediterranean countries. This research was important to my personal formation, a sort of *immersion* I did around the ages of thirty-five to thirty-seven. I got a great deal of profit from it, even though I didn't use these documents very much in my writing, except about armaments during the First World War and on the Catholic Church's attitude towards them. On the Mediterranean questions I guided the studies of some of my friends, such as Marco Impagliazzo, who has devoted his research to Monsignor Duval and the Catholic Church. He has recently published another book on the Church in Libya and the Italian occupation. Another new volume, also recently printed, is a biography of Athenagoras, the Patriarch of Constantinople.

This is a significant key to interpreting Sant'Egidio: action isn't something separate from reflection. Perhaps it's useful to mention the books and other works published under the editorship of the community by the publishers Morcelliana in Brescia in the series "Cieli aperti" (Open Heavens), which already lists various titles: the subjects covered go from ecumenical dialogue to relations with the non-Christian religions, from peace and war to immigration. Then there are other books, brought out by other publishers, Catholic and otherwise, from San Paolo to Piemme, to Rizzoli: some directly referring to the work of the Community, others that express its sensibility, although they undoubtedly bear the mark of the different authors. These books make it clear that at Sant'Egidio learning is significant.

Certainly, culture has great value. Books are a way to deepen our experience. I'm very much in favour of this relationship between culture and the community, without separation but also without confusion (that's the doctrine of Chalcedon), to the extent that, it seems to me, research has a logic all its own, which is different, in any case, from the logic of action. I don't separate the two orders, but they mustn't be confused. I surely don't believe, however, that a Christian community produces its own separate culture, a culture expressed with a language and categories that are totally "other". Strictly speaking, you can't say that Sant'Egidio has a specific culture. But I have the feeling that a community like ours sends out signals that its members, but also its friends and those closer to it or the persons with whom it engages in dialogue, can recognize. A community has to be a place of meeting. That's why I don't believe in a "Sant'Egidio culture", even if on some subjects we do have a programme and some concrete experience that can at times be original and enriching, within a larger cultural context – or, occasionally, amid a certain silence or conformism. That's also why we don't have a journal, "The Sant'Egidio Review". The place to take positions is life, the world. A review isn't a community. You can do an official bulletin, where you print speeches or information, as if it were a kind of telephone line. A review is something else again; it's a product in itself. In a word, either you do a bulletin or you invent a publication with an original identity. And that's another way of seeing the world: although then there's the risk of building not a community, but a little Church, or a more or less fundamentalist chapel. I say "fundamentalist" simply because it has the obligation to be "original" and presumptuous. On the contrary, it's necessary to dialogue with culture and with cultures, with persons. A church community like ours shouldn't, in my opinion, be its own publisher. It is what it is: it sends messages and, above all, it receives them.

In fact, the authors who belong to Sant'Egidio publish with the most diverse firms and, in some cases, free of any religious commitment of any kind.

There's no publishing house of Sant'Egidio.[4] Besides, we wouldn't have the capacity for it. I myself have published a lot with Laterza, in Bari, which has a secular tradition and which owes a great deal to Benedetto Croce: *Le Chiese di Pio XII* ("The Churches of Pius XII") in 1986, *Chiesa e papato nel mondo contemporaneo* ("Church and Papacy in the Contemporary World") (in collaboration with Giuseppe Alberigo) in 1990, *Il Vaticano e Mosca* ("The Vatican and Moscow") in 1992, *Il potere del papa da Pio XII a Giovanni Paolo II* ("The Power of the Pope from Pius XII to John Paul II") in 1993, *Intransigenza e modernità* ("Intransigence and Modernity") in 1996. It was important to strengthen ties with a major publisher.

A community mustn't let itself be "dominated" by its cultural aspects: ultimately this is a form of vanity, and it isn't always necessary. I could cite some examples of communities that have become the scene of academic discussions. But many of our members have no wish to limit themselves to an experience of this sort; they're searching, instead, for concrete action. You can be a Christian and try to live your own Christianity without, for all that, being an intellectual. I'm also afraid of the opposite, a community so inattentive to culture that it doesn't even manage to exercise charity, because charity requires culture too and, in any case, intelligence, reflection, attention.

The fact that some members of Sant'Egidio have different publishers corresponds, on the one hand, to our wish to enter into dialogue with others, but above all to the dynamics of reality, to the fact that there are, even on cultural journeys, historical, concrete, individual itineraries. We have to engage in dialogue as a community and as individuals. Sant'Egidio exists in itself and has something to say. What I can say, or what this or that member can say, is something else. Each one of us lives the spirit of Sant'Egidio in the secularity of his or her own life, in the reality of his or her existence.

You can grasp the usefulness of this when you face

questions like: "What does Sant'Egidio think about old people?" or "What is Sant'Egidio's opinion on the Third World?" You can't talk about everything. That goes for the Church and for the community. A journalist once asked me what was Sant'Egidio's position on Star Wars. I could only reply with a joke: "Sant'Egidio, our patron saint, lived so long ago that in those days he couldn't even imagine Star Wars." In the search for global answers to everything I see a temptation to fundamentalism.

Have you worked personally on Islam?

I've studied Islam out of personal interest. I haven't had direct contacts with the archives because I don't know Arabic. I've only had an indirect contact through western culture or with the help of the diplomatic archives. In answering this question I realize that it opens the problem of knowing foreign languages. Italians generally aren't polyglots. At Sant'Egidio for some years now there's been a widespread interest in languages.

In what language did the discussions about Algeria take place?

We spoke in French and Arabic. The representatives of the FIS spoke English in public, but French and Arabic in private. The text of the accord was drawn up in French. Then it was translated into Arabic, the language in which it was also distributed.

And for Mozambique?

They used Portuguese.

Does openness to the cultures of the world demand knowledge of other languages?

Mastering languages is essential. That's the advice that

we often give the younger members. In reality, when we were eighteen we weren't much inclined to learn languages, perhaps because we were in Rome, we *were* Rome.

One very important moment in the life of the Community is the evening prayer. This is an aspect that's completed by the crucial place of the Sunday eucharistic liturgy: this profound attention to the liturgy is perceived as an authentic image of the living tradition of the Church.

Yes, prayer and liturgy are closely tied together. Every evening in the prayer at Sant'Egidio different persons from the community are present, along with others who come from all over. In Rome there's a community evening prayer, in our church, and – as I've already said – in two other churches in the centre, San Bartolomeo and Trinità dei Pellegrini, which was the church of St Philip Neri. The first is located on the Isola Tiberina, between Trastevere and the old ghetto: not long ago it was entrusted to the community of Sant'Egidio. It's a church that was built at the end of the 10th century, on the site of the Roman temple of Aesculapius.[5]

The Community has made the island the centre of some public demonstrations, such as the one in memory of October 16, 1943, the date of the deportation of the Jews of Rome, or against racism and in support of the immigrants. In October 1996 the tenth anniversary of the Prayer for Peace in Assisi, it was the site of Christian ecumenical prayer on the subject, "Peace is the name of God". Its position, as an island within the city, gives it symbolic interest.[6]

We've put prayer into the heart of our life, precisely as a response to the commitments that absorb us. Today these are Algeria or Burundi; yesterday we were working on the problems of foreigners; tomorrow it will be the old people in a city that threatens to become even more inhospitable than it was yesterday. You can't say that the Community has specialized in this or that type of action

– no, the Community's commitment has been diversified, but we achieve unity when the assembly comes together to pray. I'd like to leave you with this image of Sant'Egidio: a community at prayer. When somebody tells me: "I want to get to know Sant'Egidio", I generally reply, "Then come and pray with us". Every evening the prayer concentrates on the reading of the Word of God, which gives meaning to the day that has passed.

We thought that in an adult life participation in prayer would become difficult; what proves easy for young people who are rather free is much less so for people committed to professional and family life. Still, although we never made it obligatory, the church is always packed. Furthermore, Sant'Egidio plays the role of sanctuary to some extent: many groups that are passing through Rome come to take a look, to get to know us. Many of them fit a visit to Sant'Egidio into their itinerary of Christian Rome. And ancient Rome. But not just that. So, prayer is at the same time a place of listening and invocation, a moment of welcome, of hospitality. It seems to me that this is our way, one of the principal ways that we locate ourselves in continuity with Vatican II, with *Dei Verbum*: the Word restored to the people of God. We read Scripture in the midst of common prayer; there is also a commentary, and there's a brief homily.

Where do the prayers come from? How are they chosen?

The prayers are original, drafted by one or other of us, but they're often references to some old text (for the most part, these texts go back fifteen or twenty years). But others are inspired by the Byzantine liturgy, or by texts of the Greek or Latin Fathers of the Church.

Your liturgy owes a great deal to the East. The visitor can't help being struck by the icons in the church and in the various rooms of the Community's headquarters. What do you consider important about the Eastern liturgy?

The primacy of thanksgiving, of the free gift, of the presence of God and, above all, the eschatological sense of daily life. The liturgy is the great Sabbath, the eternal Sabbath, the day on which God has invaded daily life. We live strongly the sense of the gift of the day of the Lord, on which we celebrate the mystery of his presence. The Patriarch Athenagoras, a great figure of the Orthodox pastor and 20th century Christian, for whom I feel veneration, used to say in the light of the lived experience of the eastern tradition the liturgy "protects the world and secretly illuminates it".

"Man finds there the sonship that he has lost; he draws to his life from the life of Christ, the faithful friend who shares with him the bread of necessity and the wine of rejoicing. The bread is his body, and the wine is his blood; and in this unity nothing separates us any longer from anything or anyone. What could be greater? It's the joy of Easter, the joy of the transfiguration of the universe... Now nothing can make us fear anymore. We have known the love that God has for us. We have become 'gods'. Now everything has a meaning."[7]

The primacy given to the liturgy is for us a protection against ideology. It also bears us up in the struggle against poverty: it's a source of hope and love. The poor love beautiful liturgies. For them a carefully prepared liturgy is a feast. It's the rich who would like to transform it into a salon for intellectual discussion. Poor people, sick people, old people love a feast because they have a need for joy; and their joy doesn't come from themselves, but from a moment lived in common. For this reason we give the liturgy a popular and not just a "cerebral" orientation. It has to be a feast for respecting the dignity of the people of God, and for the glory of God. And there's no leap, no break in the continuity between prayer, the liturgy, and the service of the poorest of the poor. Just as there's no leap, but a continuity, in the Gospel of Luke between the parable of the Good Samaritan (Lk 10:29-37) and the episode of Martha and Mary (Lk 10:38-42).

On the contrary, one helps to understand the other. In both cases someone chooses the better part.

For more than ten years, on Christmas day after the liturgy we've offered a huge luncheon in the basilica, which glistens for the feast. We invite to the luncheon the homeless, gypsies, men and women living alone, the poor, AIDS patients, old people. And some regular patrons of our dining hall also come there. Christmas is a difficult day, an almost impossible day, for people who are alone and poor. It threatens to be a day turned upside down, a curse rather than a blessing for those who are without means or a family. Everything is prepared in a very warm, personal manner. And I have to say that you really get the feeling that the poor are at the centre of the feast and of the Church, or rather that what we try to live every day of the year is now coming true. At Christmas, between the basilica and our other premises, around a thousand people come. This luncheon is also given in many communities outside of Rome. It's not just a matter of performing a service for Christmas, but of unbroken, year-long solidarity with persons in difficulty. Still, for Christmas we wanted to create an almost liturgical solemnity in the heart of the Church. Well, I believe that this is part and parcel of what I tried to say about the centrality of the liturgy.

Can one speak of a liturgy of the Holy Spirit, as has been said of the Orthodox liturgy?

I think so, but let's not forget that the Spirit blows where it wills; and we have to recognize the space of its action. Two main highways through which the Spirit of the Lord passes are the liturgy and love. Often with Catholics – and it's a temptation for all – there's an excessive culture of the project: you've got to have projects cooking for everything; you have to justify everything, explain everything. You cannot just spend time reflecting on yourself, and nothing more. The liturgy helps us to escape from the endless rounds of discussion and permits ourselves to be invaded by the Spirit.

Is there a Christian practice of politics? Do we have to accept Max Weber's conception of the two moralities, the morality of conviction and the morality of responsibility?

Christian politics exists, and I have met it, I could say, paraphrasing others. I was born in a country where Christian politics meant the Christian Democratic party: that was a real problem, a key problem, the subject of all the debates for forty-five years, a sort of "Italian party". But we've entered a new phase in which the Christian party no longer exists. Over and over again in my life I've asked myself the question of politics; and many other times I've asked it, along with others, at Sant'Egidio: why not get into politics? That's what flashes through my mind when I feel indignation or more than usual worry about a political or social problem. But I'm sure that in my case it would have been a mistake, not in the metaphysical sense, but because we mustn't desert other realities, like those that have to do with the Church. The Christian community and the Gospel that it's committed to bear witness to can't coincide with a party. The church community has to be broad. The Word of God is free. If at Sant'Egidio we don't just discuss religious questions, but political ones as well, politics isn't, for all that, considered the culminating point of our human experience. Often, in the Italian Catholic world, Catholic organizations used to prepare their militant young members for entering politics. Those organizations constituted the natural breeding ground where the personnel of the Christian Democratic Party in Italy was taken from. This was the case of Catholic Action: the best people in it, after a few years, launched out into *political* action. It's the story of the postwar era in our country.

I was convinced that my path was different, and that I had to work in society and in the Church. In that sense I didn't want to engage directly in political work, though at various stages of my life, I've been asked to. But everything isn't politics; I thought so even back when politics seemed to be everything: as if it were the only expression of commitment that had dignity, in '68 and the years afterwards.

This isn't an attitude of scorn for politics or for the men and women who've committed themselves to it. I think, for example, that unfortunately, as things now stand, Italy finds itself with an alarming lack of political culture and of politics as the capacity to work for broad and general interests. But, to be sure, there are so many things to do. I don't believe that a Christian politics exists. But I believe that we've got to reinforce the dialogue between politics and the world of Christians, to sensitize society to the values of which we're the bearers and witnesses. This is true even if, at times, Christians have too much nostalgia for Constantine. For a long time the right in Italy has looked for a "Christian" prince to defend Catholic interests. That explains the magnetism exercised by Mussolini on some Italian Catholics. But even with the Christian left there's been a "Constantinian" attraction to socialism. The Christian prince was identified with socialism. But the City of God can't be built on earth from secure and guaranteed religious blueprints: that would be politics in the name of God, but not the politics of God, who perhaps is laughing at our crude approximations. In that sense there are many forms of Christian fundamentalism with different political outlets... And one recurrent theme is the nostalgia for Constantine.

But the age of Constantine, historically speaking, ended a long time ago. Some Churches, like the Syrian Church or the Coptic Church, never experienced it. As Father Chenu aptly says, after Vatican II the age of Constantine is no longer among the things Christians wait for. The Church, in this sense, is all by itself and with everybody. It doesn't have a privileged relationship with the political authorities. It doesn't search for political structures to fulfil its mission. Those that it does use are different. Upon meeting the man lame from birth who begged alms of Peter and John near the gate of the temple, Peter said: "I have no silver and gold, but I give you what I have; in the name of Jesus Christ of Nazareth, walk" (Acts 3:6). Christians have something to give to the world, something that comes from the Gospel. Political and economic power aren't the only things that change or determine situations. To be sure, I have no disdain for politics, but personally I give priority to the particular demands of the service of the Gospel.

In France the Christian Democrats call themselves "democrats of Christian inspiration".

You can talk about a "Christian in politics", just as you can talk about "a Christian who's a professor". The French formula is a more tenuous and more secular way of calling oneself a Christian Democrat. By the way, I don't exclude the possibility of there being parties that match that kind of formula, "Christian inspiration". There's a great tradition of democratic-Christian political culture, and it's logical that it should continue. In some cases, in Latin America or elsewhere I thought I could observe in these parties a usefulness for getting out of difficult situations (and for avoiding tragic polarizations). Italy is a special case, since the Christian Democrats are not just *a* party, but the only Christian party; and hence, they considered themselves the party of the nation. It was at one and the same time the party of the Church and the party of the State. But the political traditions of Catholics are diverse. There's a right-wing Catholicism, with a tradition that comes from far away; there's a democratic Catholicism of Christian inspiration; there are progressive Catholics, committed to the left. Be that as it may, we have to establish a distinction between faith and political expression. To be Catholic and secular – that's our challenge. But without renouncing anything.

What are the fields where we have something to say? There are many of them. As Christians we have claims to a voice in foreign policy, for example, *à propos* international cooperation, relations between North and South, or peace. We have Christian values to propose on the subject of education. There's something to be said about life, about respect for life, from conception to the last moment: the question of abortion is of great concern to us, as is the respect owed to the life of old people, and support for those who live in grinding poverty. We have to speak up in the media, because to save democracy you have to preserve a pluralism of information. Otherwise we risk having a democracy under a guardian's care.

Still you have to be careful. Christianity doesn't need to beware of confronting concrete problems, but I'm afraid of a Christianity that's all too eager to issue rulings on everything. Sometimes I think that the great challenge of Christianity is to speak to the heart of humanity. "Everything is yours, but you are Christ's", says the Apostle.

Do you consider yourself a political person?

No. But politics interests me. It's our world.

When you act in areas that involve more than just social commitment – but there too, like Sant'Egidio – aren't you talking, in a sense, about political action?

I'm a child of '68, and I could say that everything is politics. In a certain sense that's true. But the contrary is more true. I could also answer yes to the question. In reality I don't really consider myself political, beyond the paradox that "Everything is politics". I'm convinced that when the Community of Sant'Egidio works for peace and reconciliation, it uses some political instruments; in a word, it does politics, if you will. You could say the same thing about its social work, which absorbs the greater part of our energies. To be sure, it *is* politics, concrete and noble politics, every time that this social work succeeds in becoming culture, attitudes, opposition to inhuman policies, proposals that are innovative and in any way proven to combine the arguments of political rationality with those of human dignity. You could also talk about politics by underlining the religious aspects of our life. But I believe that it's important to say that we aren't a political force and we don't act according to the logic of the political world. Still, wherever Christians live together, there always develops an energy of solidarity that has an influence on real conditions. In a way that's political action.

Is your religion about a private God or a public God?

My religion is about a God who speaks in the hidden places of the heart, but whose name is shouted on the rooftops. It's the Gospel. So he's not a private God, he's not a consumer good to guarantee my spiritual comfort. But there also exists a dimension – and it's irrepressible – that's personal, private, that's all about conversion and the heart.

You've spoken of dialogue in religious life, but isn't there a moment when dialogue stops and each person's choice is made manifest?

I haven't talked only about dialogue. Christian life is complex and can't be reduced to a single dimension. But there *is* a moment when you go for the essentials. Perhaps there are decisive moments. The assassination of Father Christian de Chergé and the other Trappist monks of Notre Dame de l'Atlas in Algeria made me reflect, more acutely than at other times, on a Christian life that ends in martyrdom, with a violent death *because* one is a

Christian. I knew Father Christian rather well: he was a friend of Sant'Egidio, he always visited us when he came to Rome; and he participated in the Prayer for Peace. We had paid a number of visits to Notre Dame de l'Atlas. During the time of his kidnapping we tried every way we could to get word about him and his confrères. After a few contacts there was a great silence. Finally, the tragic news came of the assassination of the seven monks.

Father Christian was a meek man, but very strong. His position was original vis-à-vis that of the Algerian bishops: he was in agreement with our initiative, even though he didn't go along with every feature of it. He was a monk who loved life, dialogue, meeting people. His testament is eloquent: he didn't seek out death, but neither did he renounce his mission in order to save his life. The martyr isn't a hero, but someone who won't sell off everything to continue living, just to continue living. This is a feature that makes him or her similar to Jesus. In the Garden of Olives, Jesus didn't want to die and felt anguish until death. But he didn't flee Jerusalem; instead he remained until they came to get him.

Father Christian wrote in his testament, a simple and profound document, not at all sentimental: "If it should happen to me one day – and it could be today – to fall victim to the terrorism that now seems to want to include all the foreigners living in Algeria, I would want my community, my Church, my family to remember that my life is given to God and to this country." But he adds: "I couldn't wish for such a death". And he concludes: "And you too, the friend of my last moments who won't have known what you were doing... may it be given to us to meet each other like good thieves in paradise, if God wills, the Father of us both."

When I got to know this Trappist monk, in the years when terror seemed far from Algeria, who would ever have thought of such an end? Still the monk in Father Christian lived a faith whose horizon included martyrdom. It's the condition of not a few Christians. Today in

Africa, for example, bishops, priests, Christian men and women are dying because they are believers or because they are people of peace. In some countries of the world the martyrology is growing impressively longer. Being a Christian isn't a comfortable situation. Moreover – when you think of it – this has been a fact of life in the 20th century. The century of liberty and religious freedom has had many martyrs, from eastern Europe to Latin America. John Paul II conceived the important idea of calling to mind the martyrs of our century for the Jubilee, even outside the canonical processes of beatification. Martyrdom proves – judging from the first results of this investigation – to be more of a daily reality for many Christians than may be evident.

Dying because you're a Christian is less remote than you imagine. It happens even in Italy, if we think of Father Puglisi, killed by the Mafia in 1993. He wrote: "Witnessing to Christ can also become a martyrdom... It's a short step from witness to martyrdom." It's a death not sought: the only thing sought and accepted is witness to the Gospel, with all its consequences. The example of Monsignor Romero, Archbishop of San Salvador, has been with the Community of Sant'Egidio for many years: he died as a bishop while celebrating mass. Now Father Vincenzo Paglia is working for his beatification. The martyr carries a weight of history and life: his death for the faith is part of the human condition, down to its depths. Every testimony is embodied, and you could say that there were many causes of the martyr's death. There will always be prudent people ready to give *post mortem* advice. But you can't eliminate martyrdom from the horizon of life and Christian witness.

Remembering these "martyrs" widens our Christian spectrum, which is perhaps too tranquil and self-involved to take in a neglected dimension of Christian life. At bottom our tranquil generation has also been contemporary with martyrs. If I look back, I can personally recall Christians who died because they were believers. I remember, among others, Vittorio Bachelet (a former president of Italian Catholic Action and head of the Council of Magistrates, he was assassinated by the Red Guards), who showed so much affection to the Community when it was taking its first steps. Yes, perhaps we have to recall the "martyrs" and understand better how Christian testimony knows no confines or limits.

Do you think that the Christianity of our countries is weak?

The strength of Christians isn't like that of this world. Christianity is born weak. Prayer – think of the Psalter – grows in weakness. Christians aren't afraid of weakness. Sometimes in the history of the Church this weakness gives birth to the will to emulate the powers of this world: to be strong in their way. Which is absurd. That isn't the strength of Christians. Still Christians aren't destined to be spectators of history in some languid and uncommitted fashion. There's a Christian strength, as the apostle Paul says, "When I am weak, then I am strong" (2 Cor 12:10). Thus weakness and poverty aren't conditions of weariness for Christians; rather they're the territory in which their original "strength" grows. In this perspective I often refer to the "weak strength" of Christians. We've experienced it in our work for peace, as I've already said.

Disdain for weakness and poverty puts the Church and Christians into a state of subordination and dependence on prevailing attitudes, almost reducing them to silence. That's because they have nothing else to say except to adopt the offerings of the videocracy or others. Weakness and poverty are the terrain on which to leave behind the idolatries of this world, to remove yourself from their fascination and their grip on daily life. Still, weakness and poverty don't point us to an idea, but to a very concrete reality: to the poor of history, to those who are close and those who are far away. When you speak of poverty and weakness, you can't do this in the Church abstractly, as if it were just some sort of deprivation. Talking about poverty sends us back to looking the poor and the weak in the eye. Poverty is made topical by referring to the poor who are our contemporaries.

What type of weak or poor person do you especially have in mind? At this moment which seems most significant for the Community?

There's no one emblematic abstract class of poor people. We make our way along the road and we meet the poor person, trying not to bolt straight ahead as the priest or the Levite did in the parable of the Good Samaritan. At this moment, however, I feel that the weakness and the poverty of the old speak very eloquently to our western consumerist society. Old people will increasingly be an "invasive reality". And not just because their number is growing in our societies: within every one of us there's a potential old man or woman. Old people can be taken away from their homes and thrown into institutions, but you can't eliminate the old person inside each one of us. You can't remove the old face, the old body, the old person's heart that emerges from everyone, in everyone, with time. It's like an inevitable birth. Every one of us does everything to slow down or eliminate the spectre of old age. But you can't eliminate the confrontation with the weakness that is growing or being old.

The old person represents a great contemporary paradox, namely life granted and prolonged by society. All men and women can live longer now, but their lives are useless and cumbersome. The message that gets hammered into old people is that ultimately it would be better if they got out of the way. They're no good for anything. Medicine does everything it can to keep them alive, but society tells them that they're living too long. As one old man in a hospital for chronic diseases confided in me, "What's the point of my life? Who am I living for? I wait for mealtimes like an animal, then I stare at the wall. I'm not waiting for anything anymore..." For many years the Community has felt old people as a great challenge to solidarity. Friendship and identification with them have grown over the years from the experience of accompanying them in their lives.

This accompanying is simply a response to the need for assistance. It's a fact that makes life productive. The old person represents our society's great need for company. Without company old people find it hard to live. They condemn themselves to death. It's not just a matter of kind-heartedness, but a pragmatic question. Closeness reveals the value of their lives: one grasps their strength amid the ocean of their weakness. It's a question directed to the Church: old people can express the weak strength of prayer. The existence of the old, friendship with them, their place in the Church – all this is a prophecy in a society that welcomes only people who are useful. Life isn't just a form of production.

A wholly production-oriented vision has disturbed the ecosystem: one part of the population isn't useful, so why does it continue to exist? The old are no longer few and far between, there are all too many of them. This seems to be a message of social rationality; in reality it's the way a barbarous future is being readied for everyone, a future in which life will no longer be a value or a gift. What will my tomorrow as an old person be? Is my life valuable only for what I produce and as long as I have the power to assert myself? The condition of the old person raises disquieting issues for everyone. Nobody is excluded from this, not even the richest (for the poor, old age is just one more weakness).

Old people's struggle for life is the prophecy of another conception of life. Affirming the value of their life simultaneously affirms the value of free giving and – why not? – prayer. Life is more than mere activity, it's more than profit and work; it's something complex. Young people don't need the old to find out how the world is put together. They already have television to show them that. But there's a much deeper need for old people: it's the equilibrium of a human system, a sort of ecology of all of life.

What are your prayers?

I read the Bible. I pray with the psalms. For me prayer grows out of hearing the Word of God. Scripture gives us the words and the language to pray with. Think of the Psalter: Jesus himself finds guidance in the words of Scripture. So my prayers are nourished by the Bible. But the Bible is also the response to my prayer, the prayer that has ripened in the assembly of the Church.

Moreover I'm convinced that invocation of the Lord comes out of the realities of life. Prayer is also a crying out in need, a way of overcoming our everyday powerlessness. It isn't a search for a "stopgap" God, as Bonhoeffer would have put it. But prayer is nonetheless born in tight corners, in necessity, and it feeds on them. The psalms are that too. Prayer can become an aspiration for peace, not for one's own personal success. In the apostolic catechesis reported by the Letter of James, we read: "You do not have, because you do not ask. You ask and you do not receive, because you ask wrongly, to spend it on your passions" (Js 4:2-3). At times we don't know what to ask of the Lord. It's not natural to ask in prayer, because that calls for the adult to become a child, recognizing with faith his or her weakness and need. But the poor and the needy know how to ask.

Perhaps we should take more seriously Jesus' words: "Ask, and it will be given you; seek, and you will find; knock, and it will be opened to you. For every one who asks receives, and he who seeks finds, and to him who knocks it will be opened. Or what man of you, if his son asks him for bread, will give him a stone?" (Mt 7:7-9). There's no reason to be ashamed of praying on the basis of need. In the Gospel – it seems to me that I found this out at various stages of my life – Jesus teaches us to pray constantly. His counsels are also highly concrete: "Therefore I tell you, whatever you ask in prayer, believe that you have received it, and it will be yours" (Mk 11:24).

There's another dimension that I've discovered in prayer: reconciliation. Especially in prayer for reconciliation in places where you find war, radical incomprehension, and walls of hatred that seem insurmountable to human strength. The Lord and his Spirit can speak in the depths of the heart; they can follow roads that we don't see, untangle painful situations that strike us as impossible. Prayer always puts itself into a dimension of reconciliation: it's the forgiveness of the Lord, who hears me, but also my heart that frees itself from the spirit of enmity: "And whenever you stand praying, forgive, if you have anything against any one; so that your Father also who is in heaven may forgive you your trespasses" (Mk 11:25).

I think there's a great deal of prayer in the world. Certainly there's desperation, but there's also prayer. We can't "quantify" prayer. I'm thinking of the prayer of the poor, of prisoners, of the simple, of those who can't imagine their future without terrible anguish. The old, often reduced to utter powerlessness, find in prayer the hope and strength to remain present in the world, doing something for it. Perhaps this prayer protects and animates our world more than we think.

I often discover that I'm illiterate in prayer. And my prayer is often like the prayer of so many Christian believers in the East, "Lord, have mercy!" The Liturgy of St John Chrysostom begins with a very long sequence of these invocations. They are the prayer of the community and of the Church to help me. It's the Lord who teaches us to pray. It's the Bible, which isn't a scientific textbook full of answers to our questions. It's not a compendium of the doctrines of the Church. The Gospel is like a lamp that illumines our steps, which lets us perceive God's journey through the various roads of the Bible.

We have spoken of the debt Sant'Egidio owes to eastern Christians, but is there also an inspiration drawn from non-Christian prayers, Jewish or Muslim?

There's something in the Qur'an that as a believer I find striking. Muslim prayer moves me. Jewish prayer is in some ways the mother of our Christian prayer. Christian liturgy was born in the synagogue: Jesus in Nazareth, in the synagogal prayer, is almost a model of the liturgy... But I'm convinced that prayers mustn't be mixed together. I don't like it when people insert an excerpt from the Qur'an into a Christian prayer – and neither do Muslims.

In prayer there's no Esperanto: let each person speak his or her language, all languages cry out to God. The way was pointed out by the meeting in Assisi, where everyone prayed side by side with everyone else, without this amounting to some kind of syncretism.

What does it mean when people of different religions pray together side by side?

First of all, it's not a prayer of one against the other. In the historical experience of all the religions, at various times prayer has been imbued with militarism and animosity. Being close together, in the spirit of Assisi, expresses solidarity in asking for peace and in the fact of *being* at peace. The ways of prayer are diverse, depending upon the religions. You have to accept the limits of your own identity; but the limit isn't a wall. The walls between religions don't go all the way up to heaven. Meditation accompanies dialogue, and these two things allow us to overcome limits; whereas syncretism is nothing but a vain pretence to universality, to being everything and to understanding everything.

Sometimes our culture pretends to dominate the diversities of the religious world, reducing them to an organic or omniscient vision. In this way one gets the impression of being universal without actually being so. I believe, in fact, that this is impossible. The universal man or woman doesn't exist. Everyone is himself or herself, with his or her history and roots. Still, I also believe that by going down to your deepest roots you can conceive of an opening without barriers or frontiers that block off all the others. This is the experience in which I hope I've engaged myself. In a word, the universal horizon is almost revealed better by going deeper into one's own faith, rather than by pretending to catalogue everything, intellectually dominate everything, know everything, and have an experience of everything.

And the things that make you angry?

The missed opportunities. When you have a chance to do something, you've got to do it; and yet you don't manage to. My moments of anger derive from the inertia and insensitivity of society in the face of the poor. Sometimes I fear that anger is becoming a useless polemic and that politics would be the right road, the most appropriate method. Often I'm instinctively tempted to oppose things; then I realize that opposition isn't automatically the best possible attitude. Our society is made up of crises, of invective and refusal. It's a society too much given to shouting. You have to have the maturity to go a little more deeply into things. At times becoming enraged is useful. There was a holy bishop once who used to say that all the passions must be put aside, but that you have to keep a bit of anger for the good cause.

The anger of Christ against the Pharisees and the money-changers in the Temple.

I believe in the usefulness of anger, as I said, provided that it's an evangelical indignation; but it can't justify the fact of having enemies. You can always be the object of enmity: that's life. I'd say that laughing and getting enraged are two realities, two fundamental facts. There's a need to laugh, to relativize things by laughing.

What have you learned from the poor, what have they changed in you?

In the first place, I think that they prevented, perhaps even without my realizing it, a silent barbarism from worming its way into me. By barbarism I mean a life incapable of *pietas*, of passion for others different from me. The poor have broadened my horizon and my personal world. This didn't and doesn't end where it naturally would have ended for social and cultural reasons. It's a psychic and emotional expansion and, in a certain sense, another eye to see things with.

The poor, once again, have taught me that poverty is almost never a choice, that it's almost never inevitable. The vagrants who've chosen to live on the street are a minority. But at the same time the homeless, like many people with mental problems, represent a protest against the world in which we construct our daily life and against the way in which the order of the importance of things is turned upside down.

The poor have taught me not to believe in a sham world, without poor people, and not to try to erect artificial walls between myself and suffering. Suffering and weakness were things that Jesus loved – and fought against. It's unreal to try to build islands to which the poor won't have access, hoping in this way to keep suffering at a distance. The poor have taught me not to be afraid of the poor and not to be afraid of living. Many old persons nowadays are no different from the lepers that we find in the Gospel. They have the same destiny, living on the margins, the same exhaustion, afraid of what they are and what they represent. The poor are the mirror of our weakness, even if in general we're extremely privileged by comparison with them. The company of the poor is a great medicine for learning to share with others. The poor, once again, have taught me that they don't exist as "poor people", that is, as a homogeneous category, determined by need. They're persons who have, at times tragically so, the same problems that all of us have: but accentuated, unveiled. As persons they don't just have a need for the most obvious things: the need to eat, to sleep in a warm place, to be taken care of. The poor remind me that each of us needs to be treated as a friend.

Old people, terminally ill people, people with AIDS, teach us how much life there is when only a little is left and how worthwhile it is to live it. They teach me the value of life when there's no more strength left, when you're ugly and disfigured by disease. The great emotional capacities of many mentally ill people call into question a large part of our intellectual pride and our Cartesian faith or whatever it is in us that believes it can dominate the complexity of the real world by reason. Physical handicaps are a great lesson for a society where everyone is clean, healthy, and beautiful, a society that's too narrow for the majority of us. They're a great antidote to the creation of standards that for most of the human race are too hard to satisfy.

Doesn't western man have a pronounced tendency to forget Christ? Isn't there a contradiction between the work of Sant'Egidio, so much inside the world, and that world itself, western society, which is becoming more and more indifferent to the message of Christ? What will Sant'Egidio be tomorrow in a world that forgets Christ?

There have been excellent books written on the agony of Christianity in the West. I'm thinking for example, of Jean Delumeau's *Il Cristianesimo sta per morire?* ("Is Christianity about to die?"), published in 1977. Is Christianity in the West dying? I believe neither in the usual catastrophism nor in the triumphalism of revenge. There has never been an Age of Gold, although some people have believed in it. Every generation has to live and make its choices.

It's true, Christianity in Europe is going through a difficult period. Perhaps we run the risk of having more religion than Gospel. Nowadays Christianity, among us, no longer has enemies, either obvious nor consistent ones. The absence of an enemy can make life more difficult or less clear. "What would Rome be without its enemies?" asked Cato the Elder, after the destruction of Carthage. Communism, anticlericalism, liberalism, free-masonry were difficult but openly hostile. All this has disappeared or has taken on more ordinary, less massive aspects. Which is good. We have the chance to escape the culture of the enemy that has blocked us and to enter the culture of alliance. But friendship is much harder to live than hatred for one's enemy. The culture of friend-ship is complex, while the culture of hatred is simple. That's the challenge.

The disappearance of the enemy leads to the discov-ery of indifference. This is the drama of eastern Europe. Still, the events of 1989, the fall of the communist re-gimes, were happy moments for the Church. At the time it had won an important victory and of course it took over the headlines. We entered into a difficult time, marked by the challenge of the sects and the emergence of a new generation. The old traditional, anticlerical communist culture took the Church seriously and fought it. Confronted in a very harsh and negative fashion, the Church was at least considered a real danger. Today all that is over. By no longer being the great enemy the Church loses its prominence; it becomes just another item in a sort of everyday supermarket where the shelves are all more or less the same. In this new context I wonder what evangelization means. When I see our cities with the cathedrals in the heart of town, the thought comes to me that this is just a question of archaeology, because in the poor suburbs the Church is no longer at the centre of things; and perhaps there no longer *is* a centre in personal and social life. Everyone puts in the centre what he or she wants. Today is a new era, when everything, even religion, is part of the market. But I frankly admit that I love my time, the one I was born in, without being blind to its weaknesses. I love it because it's mine. Faith isn't nostalgia or desire for flight, but waiting.

The Russian priest Aleksandr Men, who was assassinated, said that we find ourselves at the beginning of Christianity. I know that you like to quote this phrase. What does it mean?

We've shed light only on some elements of Christianity's great treasure. This can readily be seen on the issue of peace, which was barely touched on in the past, while in the course of the last few decades it's become a leading and prophetic mission of the Church. Yes, we really are at the beginning of something. Then what meaning can lie in the year 2000, which we're now approaching? The Apostle Peter says that a thousand years are like a day in the sight of the Lord; so 2000 is like two days! There are, undeniably, historic dates; and we have to welcome the year 2000 as the date of a grand revision of our Christianity. For example, if we take the knotty issue of Christian unity, how much time will it take to realize it? If we continue with this entirely theological dialogue, will we get anywhere? Patriarch Athenagoras used to say that we ought to put the theologians on an island and starve them out until they came to an agreement. This is urgent. Why not rediscover in depth the Church of the first millennium, which was undivided, in communion even when deep differences persisted? Evidently the unity of the Church doesn't mean uniformity. This is only one example, because we've already spoken of the unity of the Church.

And what should a Christian anthropology for the year 2000 be? Is it yet to be invented? In that sense, I think that experiences like those of Sant'Egidio, the experience that each one of us lives, represent a moment of travail and preparation for what the Christian of the third millennium will be, a man or woman of peace, of the Gospel, someone who will have to return to his or her roots. Vatican II has set us free, not to live as we ourselves see fit, but to build this Christianity of the beginning of the third millennium. Christianity has immense energies that we know little of, that we've done almost nothing to explore or try out. It's not an old text to be recited today and tomorrow with more virtuosity than yesterday. It's a reality to be lived profoundly. It's to be discovered, as Father Men used to say. The Spirit guides us towards the whole truth. And quite a lot of us will be able to live this. It seems to me that I know many people, even simple people, who are already living an extraordinary life and who find an unsuspected energy in Christian faith.

The millennarians are waiting for the return of Christ to earth. That's not what you're waiting for?

No, but we *are* open to the future, and we're trying to enter the next millennium. And the risen Christ will make an appointment with his disciples: in Jerusalem, in Galilee... or somewhere else.

NOTES

1 Yvan Daniel, ed., *La religion est perdue à Paris... Lettre d'un vicaire parisien à son archevêque en date de 1849, suivie d'un mémoire adressé au même* (Paris, 1978).
2 On ecumenical dialogue see A. Riccardi, "Du monde aux religions", in *Nouvelle Revue théologique*, 1991, 3, pp. 321-339. Among the other publications by Riccardi are: *Il Vaticano e Mosca* (Rome-Bari, 1993); *Un vescovo meridionale tra modernizzazione e Concilio. Enrico Nicodemo a Bari (1953-1973)*, ed. A. Riccardi (Bari, 1989); "Une école de théologie tra la Francia e Roma", in *Cristianesimo nella storia*, 1985, 5, pp.11-28; "La fortune d'une encyclique", in *Revue des Deux Mondes*, 1991, May, pp. 75-81; "La Chiesa e

Roma durante la Resistenza. L'ospitalità negli ambienti ecclesiastici", in *Quaderni della Resistenza laziale*, 1977, 2, pp. 89-150; "La grande dinamica sociale e politica dell'Africa dopo la fine della presenza politica dell'Unione Sovietica", in *Concilium*, 1992, 1, pp. 97-107; "Le religioni in un mondo secolarizzato", in *I viaggi di Erodoto* (1994), 1, pp. 207-13; "Le primat de l'évangélisation", in *Les politiques de Dieu* (Paris, 1993) pp. 99-116; "Da Giovanni XXIII a Paolo VI", in *Chiesa e papato nel mondo contemporaneo* (Rome-Bari, 1990) pp. 169-285; "Dalle Chiese di Pio XII alla Chiesa italiana", in *Un vescovo italiano del Concilio, Enrico Bartoletti 1916-1976* (Genoa, 1988) pp. 164-190; "De l'Église de Pie XII à l'Église de Jean", in *Jean XXIII devant l'histoire*, ed. G. Alberigo (Paris, 1989), pp. 128-175; "La diplomatie pontificale en Europe orientale, de la révolution bolchévique à la coexistence pacifique (1917-1978)", in *Le Vatican et la politique européenne*, ed. J. B. D'Onorio (Paris, 1994), pp. 43-84; "La Chiesa di Pio XII, educatrice di uomini e di popoli tra certezze e crisi", in *Chiesa e progetto educativo nell'Italia del secondo dopoguerra 1945-1958* (Brescia, 1988) pp. 9-36.

3 See A. Riccardi, "Coabitazione e conflitti tra religioni nel Mediterraneo", in *Il Mediterraneo nel Novecento* (Cinisello Balsamo, 1994) pp. 19-59, and "Benedetto XV e la crisi della convivenza multireligiosa nell'Impero ottomano", in *Benedetto XV e la pace – 1918* (Brescia, 1990) pp. 83-128. In this framework of interests various research projects were carried out with collaborators, friends, and colleagues, among whom it is worth pointing out R. Morozzo Della Rocca, *Nazione e Religione in Albania (1920-1944)* (Bologna, 1990); M. Impagliazzo, *Duval d'Algeria. Una Chiesa tra Europa e mondo arabo (1946-1988)* (Rome, 1994); V. Ianari, *Chiesa, coloni, Islam, Religione e politica nella Libia italiana* (Turin, 1996); V. Martano, *Athenagoras il patriarca (1886-1972). Un cristiano fra crisi della coabitazione e utopia ecumenica* (Bologna, 1996).

4 The community has seen to the publication of some books put out by Morcelliana in Brescia: *Vangelo in periferia*, ed. M. Marazziti, 1987 (translated into Spanish and Portuguese); *Stranieri nostri fratelli: Verso una società multirazziale* (1989); *Cristianesimo e Islam. L'amicizia possibile* (1989); *Oltre il mito. Gli stranieri in Italia* (1990); *Religione in dialogo per la pace* (1991); V. Vinay, *Commenti ai Vangeli* (1992); *L'ospite inatteso. Razzismo e antisemitismo in Italia* (1993); *Il dialogo non finisce. Pietro Rossano e le religioni non cristiane* (1994). One important text for knowing the work of the Community among AIDS victims is M. Marazziti, *Uno straordinario vivere. Storie di Aids, solidarietà e speranza* (Casale Monteferrato, 1990). On the Prayer for Peace see *War Never Again. Mai più la guerra. Religioni e pace* (Brescia, 1990); *Pace a Milano* (published in collaboration with the archdiocese of Milan) (Cinisello Balsamo, 1993); H. Hoet, *Pélerins de la paix. Dans l'esprit d'Assise 86* (Louvain, 1992).

5 The construction of the basilica is due to Otto II, who wanted to

honour the relics of the Apostle Bartholomew and of St Adalbert, a preacher of the Gospel and witness to the freedom of the Church in Bohemia. The crypt, perhaps dating back to before the 11th century, has been preserved along with a fresco, painted around the year 1000, of a Madonna with the child Jesus, in an eastern style. 1997 will see the celebration of the 1,000th anniversary of the martyrdom of St Adalbert, who is venerated by both the Slavic West and the East.

6   The church of Trinità dei Pellegrini, built on the other side of the Tiber from Trastevere, beyond the Ponte Sisto, goes back, in its original parts, to the end of the 15th century, and was consecrated with this title in 1616. The confraternity of the Most Holy Trinity, founded in 1548 by St Philip Neri, was occupied with taking in convalescents and poor pilgrims. In the adjoining convalescent home, during the Roman Republic, Goffredo Maeli died.

7   O. Clément, *Atenagora. Chiesa ortodossa e futuro ecumenico* (Brescia, 1995) p. 337.